In Search of York

By the Same Author
Along the Ramparts of the Tetons:
The Saga of Jackson Hole, Wyoming

IN SEARCH OF YORK

The Slave Who Went to the Pacific with Lewis and Clark

BY
ROBERT B. BETTS

Colorado Associated University Press

BOULDER, COLORADO

Copyright © 1985 by Robert B. Betts
International Standard Book Numbers 0–87081–144–4 (cloth)
and 0–87081–149–5 (paper)
Library of Congress Card Catalog Number 82–074150
Printed in the United States of America
Designed by Bruce Campbell
Typeset by Columbia Publishing Company, Inc.
Printed by Paragon Press

Colorado Associated University Press is a cooperative
publishing enterprise supported in part by Adams State College,
Colorado State University, Fort Lewis College, Mesa
College, Metropolitan State College, University of Colorado,
University of Northern Colorado, University of Southern
Colorado, and Western State College

For my wife.
And for a very old black woman I was taken to see
many years ago and told she had been the
slave of my great-grandfather.

Contents

List of Illustrations

Preface

The Lewis and Clark Expedition was the creation of Thomas Jefferson and one of his fondest dreams come true. Launched during his first administration, its purpose was to penetrate the unknown balance of the North American continent west of the Mississippi River and south of Canada by ascending the Missouri River to its source, crossing the vaguely rumored Rocky Mountains, and, in the words of Jefferson's confidential message to Congress of 18 January 1803, continuing on "even to the Western ocean."[1] The reason the message was confidential is that Jefferson was requesting permission to send a military contingent across territory then in the process of being transferred from Spain to France. By way of explanation, he said the expedition would "enlarge the boundaries of knowledge," extend "the external commerce of the U.S.," and be viewed by Spain as "a matter of indifference."[2] What he did not tell Congress, at least in the written message, is that he had already approached the Spanish ambassador with the idea and had been informed "an expedition of this nature could not fail to give umbrage to our Government."[3] Congress approved the undertaking and appropriated $2,500 to carry it out, although in the end the cost far exceeded that amount.

Throughout the winter and spring of 1803, American negotiators who had been sent to Paris to try to purchase New Orleans and the vast Louisiana Territory from Napoleon were frustrated at every turn. Then, in a sudden change of mind, he consented to the sale, and just after Captain Meriwether Lewis left Washington on 5 July 1803 to join William Clark in Kentucky, official word was received that the land they would cross from the Mississippi to the crest of the Rockies had become part of the United States.[4] The ownership of the land beyond, however, was still unresolved. Great Britain, Spain, and Russia all eyed it acquisitively,

Rembrandt Peale's portrait of Thomas Jefferson, painted in 1805. *Courtesy the New-York Historical Society, New York City.*

as did the United States, which based its claim to the so-called Oregon country upon the discovery of the mouth of the Columbia River by an American sea captain in 1792. When Lewis and Clark reached the Pacific by an overland route and wintered on its coast, they did much to anchor this claim until, years later, streams of settlers populated the region and put the matter beyond dispute.

By a combination of Jefferson's inspired planning and the remarkably gifted field leadership of Lewis and Clark, the expedition was a brilliant success. Departing from the vicinity of St. Louis on 14 May 1804, the more than forty men of the initial party laboriously worked a large keelboat and two long pirogues up the Missouri to the Mandan Indian villages in what is now North Dakota, where a bitterly cold winter was passed in a crude wooden fort they built for both protection and warmth. With the coming of spring in 1805, the final party of thirty-one men, an Indian girl, her infant son, and a Newfoundland dog headed west into a geography only Indians had ever seen, discovering as they went the Great Falls of the Missouri, the Three Forks of that river, and the forbidding fact that mountains of a magnitude no Americans had faced before blocked their path. With horses obtained from the Shoshoni Indians, they barely managed to survive the crossing of the massive Bitterroot Range and drop down to rivers which carried them to the Pacific, where they built another crude fort and spent a dismal, rain-drenched winter. The return trip was easier. In the course of it, Lewis explored farther north within present-day Montana than had been done on the outward journey, engaging in the first blood-shedding incident between Americans and members of the Blackfoot tribe, while Clark less eventfully explored the Yellowstone River. On 23 September 1806, jubilantly firing their rifles as they came, the explorers arrived in St. Louis to the amazement of the people there and throughout the nation who had long given them up as dead.

When the Lewis and Clark Expedition appeared from out of the wilderness after having traveled approximately 8,000 miles in just under two and a half years, it brought back what Bernard DeVoto has called "the first report on the West, on the United States over the hill and beyond the sunset, on the province of the American future."[5] He was referring not only to the first flash of excitement when the news of the explorers' return swept across the land, but also to the daily journals Jefferson had insisted be kept, which contained invaluable descriptions of the size and bountiful richness of the country the expedition had traversed—the prairies, rivers, mountains, valleys, natural resources, plants, animals, and Indian tribes. Largely because of these journals, the American people for the first time could begin to comprehend with a sense of detail the enormous scope of their continent and could begin to envision realistically the ultimate westering destiny of their nation. Eventually, although much more quickly than anyone could have foreseen, the land along the route taken would add eleven states to the seventeen then comprising the fledgling republic the small band served.

Under the equally shared command of Lewis and Clark, two young army officers of prominent Virginia and Kentucky families, the members of the expedition came from widely diverse backgrounds. Most were either soldiers who volunteered from garrisons west of the Appalachians or frontiersmen who were recruited in the same region, but who were originally from the South, the Middle Atlantic States, and New England as well. Several were French-speaking sons of white and Indian marriages; one was an immigrant from Germany; and still another was a full-blooded Shoshoni Indian, the legendary Sacagawea, the squaw of the French Canadian interpreter Toussaint Charbonneau.[6] As different as they all were, one stood out from the rest. His name was York—just York, nothing more, for he was a slave who had no legal right to own anything, even a last name.[7] The exceptionally large and strong body servant of William Clark (and apparently his companion from childhood), York had been born into bondage as a member of a race then thought by some to be subhuman, a race for whom it was commonplace to be bought and sold. Of them all, only he knew what it was like to be denied freedom and to have a cash value placed upon his body simply because his skin was black.

York is a man history has passed by. Instead of being remembered along with other early black Americans who took part in momentous events— such as Crispus Attucks, the first to fall in the Boston Massacre, and Salem Poor, who fought at Bunker Hill and endured the dreadful winter at Valley Forge—York is unknown to almost all blacks and whites alike. Yet, as the journals of the expedition testify, this first black man to cross the continent north of Mexico played a meaningful role in one of the most notable explorations in history.[8] Not only did he faithfully perform his share of the duties required of every member in order for the expedition to reach the Pacific, which in itself should have won him recognition, but by virtue of the color of his skin he served Lewis and Clark in two additionally important ways. To those Indians who had never seen a black person, York was a remarkable phenomenon, "big medicine" to be viewed with astonishment and awe, thereby enhancing the prestige of these white strangers who informed them their Great White Father now resided in a place called Washington. Without overstating the case, it can also be said that York's presence at a particularly critical moment helped provide the means for Lewis and Clark to continue on instead of almost surely having to turn back. When Lewis and three others went ahead of the main party in a desperate search for the Shoshonis, without whose horses the Rockies could not be crossed, the ones they met were suspicious and showed signs of running away, an eventuality Lewis feared would "defeat the expedition altogether."[9] By great good luck, word of the black man who was coming along so excited the Shoshonis' curiosity that Lewis cited York as a principal reason they stayed, thereafter becoming friendly with the explorers, providing them with horses, and helping them on their way.

If the modest niche York deserves in American history could be given him merely by reciting his contributions to the expedition, that would be easy enough to do. But the matter becomes somewhat complicated because there are two different Yorks to deal with: the York of the Lewis and Clark journals and the York of myth. Over the years, in the many books and articles which have been published about Lewis and Clark since the late 1800s, the York of myth has become the dominant figure, a man of whom more nonsense has been written than has been written of any other member of the group, including Sacagawea. He has been variously portrayed as a giant of superb physique and stamina; a buffoon who contributed nothing more than comic relief to the expedition; a man whose blackness so appealed to the Indian women that he left a trail of kinky-haired children across the West; a fluent speaker of both French and Sioux; a slave whose relationship with his master was always one of blissful harmony; and, finally, a free man who either died of cholera in Tennessee or, in the strangest story of all, somehow lived on to spend his waning years in the Rocky Mountains as an honored member of the Crow Indian tribe. As it turns out, these customary portrayals of York bear little resemblance to the man who emerges from the pages of the dependable documents in which he is mentioned. As it also turns out, these portrayals clearly reveal that with few exceptions writers have taken liberties with him they would not have dreamed of taking had his skin been white.

When the York of the Lewis and Clark journals is compared with the York of myth, a surprising fact becomes apparent. Whereas those who kept journals during the long journey to and from the Pacific never wrote a single word tainted with racial bias about their black companion, most of what has been written about him since the late 1800s has been warped by prejudice. Although in many instances this prejudice reflected the narrow thinking of earlier times rather than deliberate malice, several generations of writers gradually distorted the York of the original sources to the point where in Lewis and Clark lore he became a racial stereotype, a comic character to evoke laughter, not serious consideration. How this came about is in itself a cameo example of the way our history was for so long presented from an almost exclusively white point of view and is a secondary theme of this book. The primary purpose here, however, is to break through the stereotype and try to see York as a credible human being, a man who knew firsthand his country at its best and at its worst—from the heights of the magnificent achievement of the exploration to the depths of slavery.

This book is divided into five parts. The first traces York's participation in the expedition and is derived almost entirely from what was written about him in the journals. The second examines the myths which have sprung up around him in the light of what those who knew him specifically said and did not say, and in so doing draws a line between where the facts end and fantasy begins. The third, based upon scholarly studies of slavery and a number of previously unpublished documents, attempts to reconstruct his life as a slave, his life as a free man, and the nature of his relationship with William Clark, which, contrary to all tradition, was marred in later years by a falling out between the two men. The fourth investigates the bizarre story that a trapper in the Rocky Mountains found him living happily as a chief among the Crows after he was reported to have died of cholera in Tennessee. And the fifth, a short final chapter, brings together the sum of the knowledge the search has revealed.

While these different approaches may give the impression they in the end add up to a definitive portrait of York, the reader should not be misled. Too little was written about him while he lived and too much time has passed since he died for that to be possible. Nevertheless, when the myths are stripped away, when the depictions of him which were distorted with prejudice are judged for what they are worth, and when he is viewed in terms of what is now known about the lives of slaves in general and body servants in particular, a more rounded image of the man takes form. We can see a York much more complex than we have been conditioned to think, a York much more important to the success of the expedition than we have been told, and a York much more tragically a victim of slavery than we have been given to believe.

I

THE YORK OF THE LEWIS AND CLARK JOURNALS

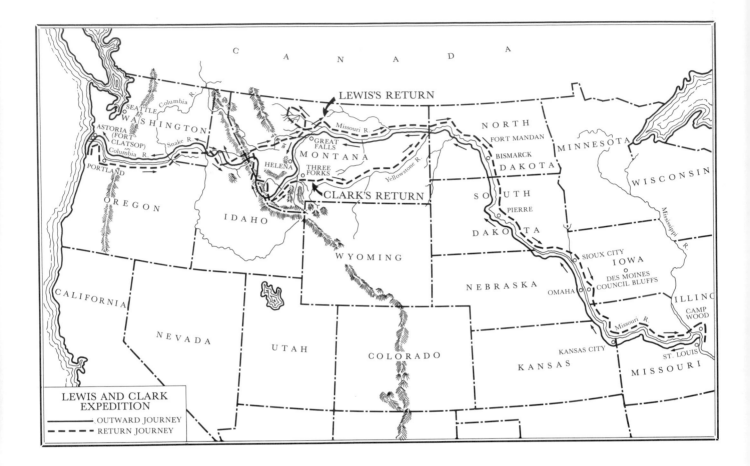

LEWIS AND CLARK
EXPEDITION
—— OUTWARD JOURNEY
- - - RETURN JOURNEY

1. To the Mandan Villages

Having served as President Jefferson's private secretary for two years, and having received from him written instructions covering every contingency it was possible to foresee, Captain Meriwether Lewis began the first leg of the long journey to the Pacific alone on 5 July 1803.[1] Leaving Washington and proceeding to the government arsenal at Harper's Ferry, he arranged to have weapons and supplies transported to Pittsburgh, then went on to that city and ordered the construction of a sail-bearing keelboat fifty-five feet long. After many vexing delays, the keelboat was finally completed on the last day of August, and with "11 hands 7 of which are soldiers, a pilot and three young men on trial" he immediately started down the Ohio River.[2] At the same time, he started to keep a journal, just as at least six others would do in the course of the actual exploration.[3]

In his journal of the trip down the river, Lewis mentions that along the way he purchased a Newfoundland dog, later identified as Scannon, but he unaccountably fails to give any description of a much more important event which took place at the Falls of the Ohio at Louisville. There he joined forces with William Clark, a friend and former army comrade who earlier had accepted Lewis's offer to share equal command of the expedition, and, while awaiting Lewis's arrival, had recruited what appears to have been at least seven young men for it.[4] There, too, Clark's slave York almost certainly came aboard the keelboat. Despite the absence of any document explicitly stating that York joined the expedition at the Falls of the Ohio, the chances of him having joined it elsewhere are virtually nonexistent. As Clark's body servant, his duty would have been to stay in close attendance upon his master. Also, when some weeks later the expedition went into winter quarters at Camp Wood on the Mississippi, opposite the mouth of the Missouri, he is named as a member of the party.

These matched portraits of William Clark (left) and Meriwether Lewis (right) were painted by Charles Willson Peale to hang in his museum of natural history in Philadelphia. *Independence Hall Historical Park Collection.*

The expedition left Louisville on October 26 and continued down the Ohio, picking up civilian and military volunteers as it went, then swung up the Mississippi and arrived at the Wood River in Illinois (at that time part of Indiana Territory) on December 12. For the last part of the trip, Clark relieved Lewis of keeping the journal, but even so York does not appear in it. While this may seem to be strange, the explanation is simply that Clark and the other journalists had so many duties to attend to they usually confined their entries to only the most significant events of the day, often leaving out the names of individuals. As an example of how sparse the journals are in terms of personal references, during the entire winter at Camp Wood, where huts were built and the men drilled into some semblance of a military command, the field notes kept by Clark on a daily basis mention York by name only three times. On December 26, he observed, "Corpl. White house & York Comce [commenced] sawing with the Whip Saws," thereby indicating that by this early date York was already working with the other men and not serving his master full-time as a body servant.[5] Months later, on 7 April 1804, York appears again when Clark describes a visit to St. Louis: "Set out at 7 oClock in a Canoo with Cap Lewis my servant York & one man at ½ past 10 arrived at St. Louis."[6] Finally, in a roster of the party prepared before leaving Camp Wood, Clark lists "2 of us & york," which perhaps can be interpreted to mean that he considered Lewis, York, and himself to be a single unit in terms of travel and living arrangements.[7]

"Under a jentle brease," the keelboat and two long pirogues crossed the Mississippi and started up the Missouri on 14 May 1804, with Clark remarking that among the more than forty members of the party were "2 Self."[8] (The editor of Clark's field notes believes the unusual phrase "2 Self" refers to Clark and York, which suggests that over the years Clark, like many other masters, had come to think of his body servant and himself as inseparable.) Not until some weeks later is York mentioned again. On June 5, he swam to a "Sand bar to geather Greens for our Dinner," one of a few references to him and food that have led several writers to say he was a cook, although the journals do not provide sufficient evidence to confirm or refute the point.[9] That York could swim is of interest only insofar as it points up the inability of some of his companions to do so. One of the puz-

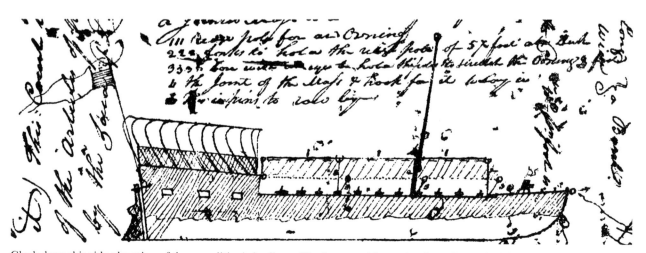

Clark drew this side elevation of the expedition's keelboat. The boat would travel only as far as the Mandan villages in North Dakota, then would return to St. Louis when Lewis and Clark and thirty-one others set out for the Pacific. *Yale University Press.*

zling questions about the expedition is why Lewis and Clark, while placing a high priority on survival skills in the recruitment of their men, selected a number who could not swim to make a journey they knew in advance would be largely on rivers.

On June 20, as the expedition was laboring upriver under oppressive heat and humidity, an entry in Clark's journal startles the reader by seeming to say that York had been the victim of an unpleasant incident, perhaps even one with ugly racial overtones. He wrote, "My Servent York nearly loseing an Eye by a man throwing Sand into it."[10] Happily, however, it turns out that prejudice was not the cause of the injury. To the contrary, Clark's field notes say the throwing of the sand was done "in fun," an important clarification revealing the incident to have been neither the result of anger nor of racial animosity.[11] The phrase "in fun" may even mean that by this time York had been accepted as one of the men, at least to the point where he could engage with them in what sounds very much like youthful horseplay. If nothing else, it surely means that in the day-to-day life of the expedition he was not socially isolated within the small community of white explorers because he was black.

As they "proceeded on," a phrase the journalists were fond of using, York either participated in or witnessed most of the adventures and misadventures befalling the expedition, although he is only now and then referred to by name. He undoubtedly was one of the "all hands" who regularly jumped into the water from the keelboat and struggled to keep it from overturning when it struck sand bars; he suffered along with the others from the plague of boils, dysentery, ticks, and mosquitoes that made life miserable along the Lower Missouri; he was on hand when punishment, usually in the form of lashings, was meted out to a few of the men who had yet to understand they were part of a military unit; and he must have stood close by when the captains held councils with the Indians, announcing to them that France had recently sold the United States the land they all along had innocently thought was their own. At these early councils, when Lewis and Clark paraded their men and gave the chiefs peace medals, the greatest object of curiosity was Lewis's noiseless, smokeless air gun, not York, for these tribes had seen black men and were unimpressed by the color of his skin. Soon, however, he would become the center of attention,

Both sides of the Jefferson Peace and Friendship Medal of 1801. Lewis and Clark gave medals like this to chiefs of the tribes they met along the way. *Courtesy of the American Numismatic Society, New York.*

viewed by more remote Indians with astonishment and awe, almost as a man from another planet.

On August 20, within the environs of present-day Sioux City, Iowa, Sergeant Charles Floyd died of what has since been diagnosed as a ruptured appendix, and in Clark's field notes York is singled out as having been particularly attentive to him.[12] What he did to ease the young sergeant's last hours is not enlarged upon, nor is he mentioned again until four days later, when Clark says he shot an elk. While this first reference to York bearing arms comes as something of a surprise in view of statutes prohibiting slaves from having knowledge of guns, what is especially surprising is that York seems to have been more proficient with his weapon than can be readily explained on the grounds that he had been trained to use it at Camp Wood. Just a few weeks later, when shooting buffalo was still a new experience, Clark wrote, "in the evening after the boat landed, I Derected My Servent York with me to kill a Buffalow near the boat from a Numb'' then Scattered in the Plains," not the easiest of tasks for a novice marksman.[13] Perhaps York had been trained at Camp Wood and was a naturally good shot; it is certainly a possibility. But what seems more likely is that he had been familiar with firearms for years, having been one of those trusted slaves who were granted exemptions from the statutes if they lived along the frontier (as the Clark family had after it moved from Virginia to Kentucky) and their owners applied to a justice of the peace for a license allowing them to carry weapons.[14] Whatever the case, after shooting the elk and the buffalo, York's name recurs with regularity throughout the journals in connection with bringing down game.

When Indians told the captains that Spirit Mound in South Dakota was inhabited by ferocious devils "in human form with remarkable large heads; and about 18 inches high," they had to see for themselves.[15] With a small group that included York and the dog Scannon, they set off on a hot morning late in August. After seven miles, Scannon tired and was sent back, but the rest went on and finally reached the top of the mound, where, after discovering no little devils dwelling there, they looked out over a far-horizoned country few Americans even knew existed. As Clark sketched the view, "we beheld a most butifull landscape; Numerous herds of buffalow were Seen feeding in various directions; the Plain to North N.W. & N.E. extends without interuption as far as Can be seen."[16] Later, in his field notes of the day's events, Clark made a comment which has almost entirely been overlooked by those who have written about York. Describing him in terms totally at odds with his traditional image of having been a giant of superb physique and stamina, Clark wrote, "we returned to the boat at Sunset, my servent nearly exosted with heat thurst and fatigue, he being fat and un accustomed to walk as fast as I went was the cause."[17] While these words raise a question as to why a flabby and less-than-fit York was allowed to accompany a party of men who had been handpicked for their ability to withstand the rigors of the wilderness, it can be said that throughout the rest of the exploration there is not a single reference to him having been either fat or out of condition.

Late in September, as the expedition advanced farther up the Missouri, Lewis and Clark found their path blocked by the Teton Sioux, a bullying band who intimidated other tribes and exacted tribute from the few river traders venturing this far. Subjected to rude treatment and excessive demands for trade goods, the explorers came within an eyelash of open conflict when the Indians seized the rope of a pirogue to prevent it from returning to the keelboat. Clark, who was on shore at the time with several men—one of whom was probably York, for they were usually together—

George Catlin, who visited the Upper Missouri in the 1830s, painted this picture of the Teton Sioux celebrating a victory with a scalp dance. *National Museum of American Art, Smithsonian Institution.*

described the tense moment graphically: "the 2ᵈ Chief was verry insolent both in words & justures (*pretended Drunkenness & staggered up against me*) declareing I should not go on, Stateing he had not receved presents sufficient from us, his justures were of Such a personal nature I felt My Self Compeled to Draw my Sword (*and Made a Signal to the boat to prepare for action*) at this Motion Capᵗ Lewis ordered all under arms in the boat, those with me also Showed a Disposition to Defend themselves and me."[18] Despite being confronted by about one hundred excited warriors who had strung their bows and cocked their guns, the redheaded captain and those with him on shore faced the Indians down. Seeing that these determined strangers were ready to fight, the head chief ordered the men who had seized the rope to release it, and from then on, although Lewis and Clark remained wary of their intentions, the Teton Sioux made overtures designed to give the impression they were friendly.

Unlike the Teton Sioux, the Arikaras in South Dakota were genuinely friendly. They greeted the explorers with open arms and, in the case of York, with open-mouthed astonishment, for "this nation never Saw a black man before"[19] They called him "the big Medison [medicine]," a term reserved for phenomena which could not be explained; "all flocked around him & examin[d] him from top to toe"; and, according to Sergeant Ordway, "the children would follow after him, & if he turned towards them they would run from him & hollow as if they were terrefied, & afraid of him."[20] All in all, York seems to have put on quite a show, telling the Indians as a joke that he had been a wild animal until caught and tamed by his master, then performing feats of strength to convince them of the claim. From this single episode a legend has arisen to the effect that York was the wag and wit of the expedition, keeping the men in laughter from the beginning of the journey to the end, although there are good reasons to doubt its accuracy. Nonetheless, both his blackness and his strength did cause a sensation with the Arikaras, and it may be their awed reaction to him also caused Lewis and Clark to realize for the first time that in York they had a valuable asset for dealing with the unknown Indian tribes they would meet farther on.

While the Arikaras were unusual in abstaining from the use of hard liquor, they followed the custom of many western tribes of showing hospitality to their guests by offering them squaws. In his journal, Clark says these offers were refused, but he was being less than candid. During an interview in 1810 with Nicholas Biddle, who would write a narrative version of the expedition's journals, Clark told him, "Ricara women better looking than the Scioux—both are lech[er]ous and the men by means of interpreters found no difficulty in getting women."[21] Clark also told Biddle about an Arikara husband inviting York to his lodge, presenting him to his wife, then standing guard outside the door until an appropriate amount of time had elapsed, meanwhile turning away one of York's companions who

One of the Mandan villages with its earth-covered lodges, as seen by George Catlin in the 1830s. *National Museum of American Art, Smithsonian Institution.*

had come looking for him.[22] In his narrative, Biddle related both this story and another, neither of which appears in any of the journals kept in the field. While still among the Arikaras, he wrote, "such was their desire to oblige us that two very handsome young squaws were sent on board this evening, and persecuted us with civilities," going on to say, "The black man York participated largely in these favors."[23] From these two occasions reported only by Biddle—for the original journals do not mention York even once in terms of sexual activities—writers of fiction and nonfiction alike have magnified him into a dusky paramour who was the heart's desire of Indian maidens from the Mississippi to the Pacific. That in Lewis and Clark folklore York has been made a stereotype of black virility evidently has more to do with an entrenched racial cliché than with any established facts.

By the time the expedition left the Arikaras in the middle of October, the journey had taken longer than expected. Clark had once optimistically estimated they would reach the "rock Mountains" before winter struck, but now the leaves were falling fast, the nights were growing cold, and they were beginning to encounter the first early snows of the northern Plains.[24] Moving up to the junction of the Knife and Missouri Rivers in North Dakota, on October 26 they arrived at the Mandan villages, a settlement occupied by several tribes living in circular lodges covered with earth and visited occasionally by British traders from Canada. Here they built a wooden structure they named Fort Mandan and here they spent the winter of 1804–1805, having traveled by Clark's calculations some 1,600 miles up the Missouri. With an uncharted wilderness extending more than half a continent west from their little outpost, their odyssey had barely begun.

2. To the Continental Divide

The Indians at the Mandan villages were duly impressed by the many wonders the white men displayed: the keelboat, Lewis's air gun, a mill for grinding corn, and, of course, York, who again was viewed as "great medison."[1] Word of him traveled through the various villages to where the more warlike Hidatsa tribe lived, eventually piquing the curiosity of their one-eyed chief, Le Borgne, who perhaps because of his pro-British leanings did not visit the Americans at their fort until three months after it was built. Unable to contain his curiosity any longer, he finally paid a call Nicholas Biddle later described in these words:

> In the course of the conversation, the chief observed that some foolish young men of his nation had told him there was a person among us who was quite black, and he wished to know if it could be true. We assured him that it was true, and sent for York. Le Borgne was very much surprised at his appearance, examined him closely, and spit on his finger and rubbed the skin in order to wash off the paint; nor was it until the negro uncovered his head and showed his short hair, that Le Borgne could be persuaded that he was not a painted white man.[2]

Biddle does not say whether the color of York's skin made Le Borgne think more respectfully of the Americans than he had before, but at least he had seen a marvel the traders from Canada did not possess. Biddle also does not say how York reacted to Le Borgne's crude examination of his person. Perhaps he was amused; perhaps by this time he took the natives' curiosity about his skin as a matter of course; or perhaps he was outraged. As is so often the case with this slave who never left behind a single word written by his own hand, his feelings can only be surmised. There is, however, a Nez Perce legend to the effect that a similar examination months later made York's temper flare. Having grown tired of being rubbed with moistened fingertips, he is said to have seized a knife and, as the Nez Perces tell it, "make big eyes much white in eyes and look fierce at Chief."[3] If this

Although this painting by Charles M. Russell has often been called *Lewis and Clark Meeting the Mandan Indians*, the museum owning it says the correct title is *Captain William Clark of the Lewis and Clark Expedition Meeting with the Indians of the Northwest*. York is prominent in the picture. *Courtesy of Sid Richardson Collection of Western Art, Fort Worth, Texas.*

is what happened, who can fault him for at last losing his patience?

Shortly after arriving at the Mandan villages, Lewis and Clark made a decision which would lead to an obscure young Indian woman becoming one of the most honored women in American history. They hired as an interpreter a bumbling, middle-aged French Canadian named Toussaint Charbonneau, who had taken as one of his squaws a Shoshoni girl the Hidatsas had abducted while still a child during a raid into the Rocky Mountains in the summer of 1800. She was Sacagawea, and although she would not guide the captains across the West, as so many books, articles, and motion pictures have persuaded the public she did, she would prove to be a helpful and devoted member of the expedition.[4] Having been "sold as

Sacagawea, from a drawing by Edgar S. Paxon. Although the Shoshoni girl did not guide Lewis and Clark to the Pacific, as is commonly believed, she did contribute to the success of the expedition in a number of important ways. *From O. D. Wheeler, The Trail of Lewis and Clark.*

a slave to Chaboneau, who brought her up and afterward married her," she was the only member of the party who could speak Shoshoni, the language of the tribe from whom Lewis and Clark hoped to purchase horses to carry their men and supplies over the mountains they knew lay across their path.[5] She also was the only member of the party who could have shared with York any understanding of how it felt to be the property of another person.

Early in December, with the thermometer reading twelve degrees below zero, Clark led fifteen men on a buffalo hunt to replenish the garrison's dwindling meat supply. York accompanied his master and suffered from the bitter cold. At the end of the day, Clark entered in his journal: "several men returned a little *frost bit*, one of [the] men with his feet badly frost bit my Servents feet also *frosted* & his P___s a little."[6] Although Clark does not subsequently give any details about York's recovery, except to say all the frostbitten men were doing better, he does inform us that by New Year's Day York was able to join a group who had gone to the nearest Mandan village, where the chiefs asked them to dance. Clark's description of this festive gathering of soldiers and savages tells us that York was unusually agile for a man of his size. "I ordered my black Servent to Dance," he noted, "which amused the Croud Verry much, and Somewhat astonished them, that So large a man should be active."[7] A few weeks later, Clark mentioned York for the last time while still at Fort Mandan. When one of Charbonneau's squaws became ill (most likely Sacagawea, who was in the last stages of pregnancy), he wrote, "I ordered my Servent to give her Some froot Stewed and tee at dif.ᵗ times."[8]

Throughout the winter, Lewis and Clark interrogated the Indians about the country to the west, obtaining mainly from the far-ranging Hidatsas a remarkably accurate picture of the Missouri's course to where it rises in the Rocky Mountains. Meanwhile, many of their men spent their spare hours in less instructive ways. They danced to entertain the Indians and, in turn, were entertained by them, for, as Clark remarked, venereal disease was "communicated to many of our party at this place—those favores bieng easily acquired."[9] One of the more memorable events of the long, cold winter occurred when Sacagawea gave birth to a fine boy, little Jean Baptiste, who would become the apple of Clark's eye, later to be affectionately called "my boy *Pomp*."[10] He was born on February 11, just two months before the expedition started for the Pacific, and because his mother could speak Shoshoni this unweaned infant became one of the most unlikely members of any group in the history of exploration.

During the following weeks, many preparations were made. The keelboat was readied for its return to St. Louis (aboard would be a letter from Lewis to Jefferson, as well as specimens of wildlife for him to examine); six dugout canoes were built to go upriver with the two shallow-draft pirogues; and those who would make the attempt to cross the continent were pared down to thirty-three in all, including York. On 7 April 1805, the thick ice having broken in the river and geese having been flying north for several weeks, Lewis marked the historic moment of departure with these words: "we are now about to penetrate a country at least two thousand miles in width, on which the foot of civilized man had never trodden; the good or evil it had in store for us was for experiment yet to determine, and these little vessels contained every article by which we were to expect to subsist or defend ourselves."[11]

Between the abandoned Fort Mandan and the Great Falls of the Missouri, York is specifically identified in the journals only twice, which is more than some and less than other members of the party. Even though the journalists were "the writingest explorers of their time," as Donald Jackson has called them, their entries of events frequently omitted the names of the participants, leaving the reader in the dark as to the individuals involved.[12] In much the same manner, they only tersely and with stark understatement described the many dangers now being encountered. While moving through virgin country where game was so incredibly plentiful and unaccustomed to man that "Some of the party clubbed them out of the way," Lewis rather casually mentions "many hairbreadth escapes" from massive sections of the river's banks caving in and almost swamping the boats.[13] Not much later, Charbonneau, who was at the tiller of a pirogue when a sudden squall struck its sail, lost his head and nearly capsized the craft with his wife, child, and others on board. One night the top of a

The journal of Sergeant Gass, first published in 1807, was illustrated with quaint drawings such as this. Here a grizzly that looks more like a dog than a bear has treed Private McNeal. *Rare Books and Manuscripts Division, The New York Public Library, Astor, Lenox and Tilden Foundations.*

burning tree fell on Lewis and Clark's tepee and, had it not been for an alert sergeant of the guard, they would have been "crushed to attoms."[14] Both captains almost stepped on rattlesnakes, and almost every member of the party had at least one close call from that most fearsome of all western animals, the grizzly bear. (Lewis at first underestimated the ferocity of the grizzly, but soon changed his mind and wrote, "these bear being so hard to die reather intimedates us all; I must confess that I do not like the gentlemen and would reather fight two Indians than one bear.")[15]

In one way or another, York shared in all of these experiences, but not until May 29 is a clear reference made to him. Then a number of men (he probably one of them) were almost trampled in their sleep by a buffalo running back and forth through the camp after having crossed the river and having walked over a pirogue, badly bending a rifle that lay in it. Although the rifle "belonged to Capt. Clark's black man, who had negligently left her in the perogue," neither Lewis nor Clark reprimanded York for his carelessness.[16] In his journal entry, Lewis dismissed the incident by expressing gratitude that no one had been injured, and Clark did not even take the time to write down the name of the rifle's owner. The hero of the incident was the dog, Scannon. When the confused buffalo charged in the direction where the two captains were sleeping, he turned it aside and drove it out of camp.

Soon Lewis and Clark had to make a crucial decision, and in doing so York was called upon to play a part. Coming to a large fork in the river, where, from their understanding of what the Indians at the Mandans had told them, they were surprised to find one, they had to determine which was the true Missouri and which a tributary that might take them far off course. By a process of deduction since characterized as "unsurpassed in the annals of exploration in the New World," they decided the Missouri flowed in from the southwest.[17] But the matter was too important to be left to deduction alone. A reconnaissance was needed, so Lewis with six men went up the fork flowing in from the northwest (he would name it the Marias), while Clark with five men went up the fork flowing in from the southwest. Within a few days, they both came to the conclusion that their initial reasoning had been right.

The caliber of the men Lewis and Clark chose to accompany them on the

In Olaf Seltzer's *Captain Lewis at the Black Eagle Falls, June 13, 1805*, Lewis wearing buckskins and York a tricorn hat look down upon one of the five cataracts forming the Great Falls of the Missouri. *The Thomas Gilcrease Institute of American History and Art, Tulsa, Oklahoma.*

reconnaissance says much about York's standing in their eyes, especially when one realizes that even though no Indians had yet been met, signs of tribes believed to be hostile had been seen. Of the eleven men selected, two were sergeants and most of the others would come to be counted among the expedition's more reliable members. Worthy of note is that in Clark's small group was "my black man york," clearly a vote of confidence in York's dependability in the event of an attack.[18] Also worthy of note is that upon their return, after having killed three grizzlies along the way, Clark wrote, "My self and party much fatigued haveing walked constantly as hard as we could march over a Dry hard plain, decending & assending the steep river hills & gullies."[19] Since no mention is made of York not being able to keep up, as had been the case the day Spirit Mound was visited, it can be assumed that by now he had trimmed down and was in good condition.

Caching one of the pirogues at the mouth of the Marias, the explorers pushed on to the Great Falls of the Missouri, well within sight of the snow-capped Rockies. There, while Sacagawea recovered from a severe illness and the second pirogue was cached, wheels were cut from the trunks of cottonwood trees and attached to the dugout canoes so they could be transported overland eighteen miles to above the five roaring cataracts. On June 21, the grueling portage began. By the end of the next day, the captains knew that all of their men, including York, would be needed to complete the task, for Clark made no exceptions when he wrote, "we deturmine to employ every man cooks & all on the portage after to day."[20] Despite sails being raised on the dugouts to take advantage of the wind—"this is Saleing on Dry land in every sence of the word"—the portage became by far the most exhausting ordeal of the expedition to this point.[21] As Lewis observed, paying tribute to the men's stamina and morale, "at every halt these poor fellows tumble down and are so much fortiegued that many of them are asleep in an instant; in short their fatiegues are incredible; some are limping from soreness of their feet, others faint and unable to stand for a few minutes, with heat and fatiegue, yet no one complains, all go with cheerfullness."[22]

By now most of the men were nearly naked, their clothing having rotted from often being wet during the journey up the river from the Mandan villages. When a tremendous storm caught them in the open along the route of the portage, they had neither protection for their bodies nor places to hide, so they were brutally battered by the elements. Clark describes hailstones so large and wind so violent that the men "were much brused, and some nearly killed," with one man knocked down three times and others having their heads bloodied.[23] Although York was exposed to the same storm, we know he was not helping with the portage at this particular moment. Instead, he was frantically searching for his master and the Charbonneaus, who were in grave danger of losing their lives.

On the day of the storm, Clark, accompanied by York, Charbonneau, and Sacagawea with her baby son, set out to find some notes he had previously lost along the river. As they approached the largest of the five falls, York left the group to hunt buffalo on a treeless plain, and not much later Clark and the Charbonneaus, seeing a large black cloud coming toward them, took shelter in a deep ravine. So heavy was the rain and hail that suddenly a torrent of water tumbling rocks ahead of it came plunging

Charles M. Russell's drawing of Clark, Sacagawea, and her husband, Toussaint Charbonneau, es-
caping from the sudden flood in the ravine at the Great Falls. *From O. D. Wheeler, The Trail of Lewis
and Clark.*

down through the ravine, threatening to sweep them "into the river just
above the great cataract of 87 feet where they must have inevitably per-
ished."[24] Only by reacting swiftly was Clark able to get the Charbonneaus
and himself up to solid ground, where he found York looking for them. Not
having seen them enter the ravine just before the storm struck, York had
disregarded his own safety to search for them even while the storm was at
its height. (In Lewis's words, "when this gust came on he returned in surch
of them & not being able to find them for some time was much al-
larmed.")[25] Never one to dwell on emotional scenes, Clark gives us only a
glimpse of what the reunion was like when York came upon his master and
the Charbonneaus shaken but unharmed. With characteristic understatement, he merely says, "we at length reached the top of the hill safe where I
found my servent in serch of us greatly agitated, for our wellfar."[26] Then,
because all were wet and cold, Clark had "the party to take a little spirits,
which my servent had in a canteen."[27]

Charles M. Russell's sketch of Lewis and Clark at the Three Forks of the Missouri. York, with a rifle over his shoulder, can be seen between the two foreground figures. *From a print produced by the Naegele Printing Co., Helena, Montana.*

The portage was finally completed on July 2, but the journey up the Missouri did not resume until thirteen days later. The men had to dress and sew deer and elk hides to clothe themselves and two more dugout canoes had to be built when Lewis's iron-framed boat, brought in sections all the way from the government arsenal at Harper's Ferry and covered here with skins, bitterly disappointed him by failing to stay afloat. During this time, York became sick and Clark gave him "a dost of Tarter," meaning a dose of tartar emetic.[28] Whatever was wrong with him, the treatment worked, because the entry Lewis made in his journal for the same day tells us "he was much better in the evening."[29] Overall, York seems to have enjoyed good health during the twenty-eight months of the exploration, with the journals taking notice of him being indisposed only five times. By way of contrast, the journals cite numerous instances when Clark was either sick or not feeling up to par.

Shortly after arriving at the Great Falls, Clark had written, "We all believe that we are about to enter on the most perilous and dificuelt part of our Voyage," and he had already been proved right about the difficult part by the portage.[30] Now the continuing journey by water also became more difficult. As they approached the mountains, the Missouri grew increasingly shallow and swift, requiring the men to strain to advance the boats by pushing from within them on long poles or by pulling them forward with elkhide towlines while walking on the bruising stones of the river's banks and bed. As for the perils Clark foresaw, he was referring both to the rugged Rockies looming ahead (mountains that made the Appalachians back home look diminutive) and to the imperative need to make contact with the Shoshoni tribe, of whom they did not know "whither to calculate on their friendship or hostillity."[31] Because the Shoshonis owned horses the expedition had to have if it were to cross the mountains and reach the Pacific, on July 18 Clark went ahead by land to try to find them, taking with him York, John Potts, and Joseph Field. This was the second time York had been chosen as a member of a small scouting party that risked running into hostile Indians, and while there is some reason to believe he was selected partly because his color might fascinate the Indians and make them easier to deal with, there can be no doubt he was counted on to hold his own in the event of a skirmish.[32]

Covering about seventy-five miles in five days, the four men's feet became so sore from being cut by sharp stones and pierced by the needles of prickly pears they at times were "Scerseley able to march at a Slow gate," with Clark at one point remarking, "my man York nearly tired out."[33] Nevertheless, York kept going despite his fatigue, and two days and many miles later he was sent off to hunt while Clark himself "lay by & nurs my feet."[34] After rejoining the main party for one night, Clark and five men once more went in search of the Shoshonis while York stayed with the boats, and again Clark was unsuccessful. During his absence, the main party continued up the Missouri and Lewis continued a practice both captains had of naming geographical features for members of the group. On July 23 he named a creek for Joseph Whitehouse, and on July 25 he named another creek for Patrick Gass, but in his daily entries he did not name a cluster of islands they passed in the river between the two creeks. These, however, appear as "Yorks 8 Islands" in Clark's record of distances along the Missouri, printed in tables by Reuben Thwaites in a separate volume of his edition of the journals.[35] How they came to be named is not clear, although Clark probably saw them from the shore and decided then or later to give them his body servant's name. Why he chose to single out York

Charles M. Russell's *Captain Lewis, with Drewyer and Shields, Meeting the Shoshoni Indians, August 13, 1805*. Lewis, holding the flag, is being embraced in what he called the Shoshoni "national hug." *From the personal collection of Mr. and Mrs. John Di Tommaso.*

for this recognition is unexplained. The only remark opposite "Yorks 8 Islands" in the table is "W.C. on land York tired."[36]

Meeting Lewis and the boats at the Three Forks of the Missouri, where the converging rivers were named the Jefferson, Madison, and Gallatin, Clark changed places with his friend and partner in command. He now took charge of the boats, heading them up the Jefferson, while Lewis with three men went forward deep into the mountains in what was becoming a desperate search for the elusive Shoshonis. Just a few days earlier, Lewis had confided to his journal his growing concern: "if we do not find them or some other nation who have horses I fear the successfull issue of our voyage will be very doubtfull or at all events much more difficult in it's accomplishment."[37] Like Clark, Lewis and his men made two attempts to find the

Shoshonis. On the second, they saw an Indian on horseback who fled when they approached, and a day later they crossed the Continental Divide at Lemhi Pass only to return and continue the search. The next day, August 13, after seeing three more Indians who fled, they surprised two women and a girl when they came upon them not far from a Shoshoni village. The tribe that held the key to the expedition's future had at last been found.

To assure the frightened women they meant no harm, Lewis gave them trinkets and painted their cheeks with vermilion as a sign of peace. He also showed them something they had never seen before, white skin. Rolling up his sleeve, he demonstrated the "truth of the ascertion that I was a white man for my face and ha[n]ds which have been constantly exposed to the sun were quite as dark as their own."[38] While this was going on, the Shoshonis at the village were alerted to the arrival of the strangers, and suddenly sixty or so armed warriors on horseback came racing toward Lewis and his three men. But any fears Lewis may have had about their intentions were soon allayed. When the women showed the presents they had been given and told the chief who these men were, the four Americans were embraced by all, becoming "besmeared with their grease and paint," as Lewis wrote, "till I was heartily tired of the national hug."[39]

Lewis and Clark had now achieved two of their objectives: they had reached the Continental Divide and they had met Indians who owned horses. They were, however, still a long way from the Pacific (how far and how difficult the journey would be they did not realize) and the Shoshoni horses were not yet in their hands. Only after several very touchy moments, in one of which York's presence as a member of the expedition had much to do with the outcome, would they be able to press on.

In J. K. Ralston's *Into the Unknown*, Clark and the main party with the dugout canoes have arrived and are being greeted by the Shoshonis. Although he cannot be seen clearly, York is being examined by curious Indians in the right background. *National Park Service, Jefferson National Expansion Memorial.*

3. To the Pacific

After the customary ritual of smoking a peace pipe had been observed, the chief of this Shoshoni band, Cameahwait, escorted the Americans to the nearby village. There they saw hundreds of fine horses and learned that the villagers were short of food, having only berries to eat. Although the Indians shared the berries with Lewis and his men and in other ways showed every sign of being friendly, Lewis was quick to size up the situation as not entirely free of danger. He knew he was dealing with a primitive people who, as he put it, "never act but from the impulse of the moment" and "have been accustomed from their infancy to view every stranger as an enimy."[1] How right he was became apparent a few days later when the Indians who were about to go with him to meet Clark and the main party coming up with the boats suddenly balked, warning the chief that these white strangers were decoys sent by their enemies to lure them into an ambush. Despite Cameahwait saying he did not believe this and haranguing his tribesmen into making the trip, they remained suspicious, and the tension mounted when they all arrived at the place Lewis had told them Clark and the others would be and no one was there.

Lewis slept but little while waiting for Clark to appear. Expressing his mounting anxiety about the Shoshonis' intentions, Lewis wrote:

> I knew that if these people left me that they would immediately disperse and secrete themselves in the mountains where it would be impossible to find them or at least in vain to pursue them and that they would spread the allarm to all other bands within our reach & of course we should be disappointed in obtaining horses, which would vastly retard and increase the labour of our voyage and I feared might so discourage the men as to defeat the expedition altogether.[2]

The Shoshonis were nervous, and so was Lewis. Desperately, he resorted to a number of stratagems to keep them from scattering with their horses. Hoping to convince them that they were not being led into an ambush, he put on some articles of Indian clothing which made him look like one of them, gave his cocked hat to Cameahwait to wear, and even went so far as to hand the chief his gun and tell him "if I deceived him he might make what uce of the gun he thought proper or in other words that he might shoot me."[3] He also told the Indians he would be generous with the trade goods being carried in the boats and that Sacagawea, one of their people, was with the main party. But the Shoshonis still showed signs of running away, and it seems to have been only a casual mention of York that tipped the scale and kept them in place until Clark arrived.

After observing that the fate of the expedition now depended "in a great measure upon the caprice of a few savages who are ever as fickle as the wind," Lewis wrote: "some of the party had also told the Indians that we had a man with us who was black and had short curling hair, this had excited their curiossity very much, and they seemed quite as anxious to see this monster as they wer[e] the merchandize which we had to barter for their horses."[4] Nicholas Biddle, in his narrative version of the journals, goes even farther than Lewis to say the Shoshonis "seemed more desirous of seeing this monster than of obtaining the most favorable barter for their horses."[5] While Biddle seems to have expanded on Lewis's words to make York more important than the trade goods, he did receive firsthand reports about the expedition from Clark and George Shannon, and he could have heard this from them. Either way, however, it is clear that York was a principal reason the Shoshonis did not vanish with their horses, leaving Lewis and Clark staring hopelessly at the towering mountain barrier ahead.

When Clark came up with the boats, York turned out to be only one of many marvels that made the Shoshonis gape. To these Indians who had never seen white men, let alone a black one, "every article about us appeared to excite astonishment in ther minds; the appearance of the men, their arms, the canoes, our manner of working them, the b[l]ack man york and the sagacity of my dog were equally objects of admiration."[6] (Scannon's "sagacity" probably means the big Newfoundland had been trained to do tricks.) Shortly after Clark and the main party had been greeted by the Shoshonis, a stunning coincidence occurred. Called upon to translate for the captains, Sacagawea discovered that Chief Cameahwait was none other than her brother, whom she had given up all hope of seeing after her abduction by the Hidatsas five years earlier. This reunion, along with Lewis and Clark's practice of dealing fairly with Indians, did much to win the Shoshonis' friendship, and gradually enough horses were purchased to carry all of the expedition's supplies and even some of its members.

While the last of the horses were being acquired, Clark reconnoitered the canyon of the Salmon River as a possible way to get through the mountains they faced. Instead, he found the river's raging white water and the canyon's steep walls to be impassable, so he and Lewis decided to travel north to what would later be known as the Lolo Trail, an Indian route running east and west through the Bitterroot Range. On August 30, led by an old Shoshoni guide they nicknamed Toby, the explorers resumed their march, unaware that on this leg of their journey they would have to traverse one of the most forbidding parts of the Rocky Mountains. Sergeant Gass's journal all but says that York was not assigned a horse and was among those who started on foot. At least he was walking two days later when the party was passing through hilly country, for Gass wrote, "Capt.

Charles M. Russell's *Lewis and Clark Meeting the Flatheads at Ross' Hole* is considered by many to be one of the artist's greatest works. York is the diminutive figure standing by the horses on the extreme right. *Montana State Capitol, Courtesy of the Montana Historical Society.*

Clarke's blackman's feet became so sore that he had to ride on horse-back."[7] After this, the journals fall silent with regard to York, even failing to include the usual references to him astonishing the Indians when a band of Flatheads was met in Ross's Hole. Legends of this tribe, however, say he made a big impression. One has the Flatheads amazed by his strength and another has them thinking his blackness was a sign of outstanding courage in battle. The latter story, as it has come down through the years, says:

> One of the strange men was black. He had painted himself in charcoal, my people thought. In those days it was the custom for warriors, when returning home from battle, to prepare themselves before reaching camp. Those who had been brave and fearless, the victorious ones in battle, painted themselves in charcoal. When the warriors returned to their camp, people knew at once which ones had been brave on the war-path. So the black man, they thought, had been the bravest of this party.[8]

Obtaining additional horses from the Flatheads, the expedition continued north to the vicinity of present-day Missoula, Montana, where it headed west and began to climb up into the Bitterroots. From this point on, the journalists' entries for the next two weeks are devoted almost exclusively to the struggle to survive. Lack of food, bad weather, and the maze these huge, densely wooded mountains form turned the crossing into a nightmare. Horses fell and rolled down hills, smashing their packs; an early snowfall of six to eight inches made Clark as "wet and as cold in every part as I ever was in my life"; game was so scarce "we were compelled to kill a Colt for our men & Selves to eat"; sheer precipices had to be navigated at great risk; and throughout the ordeal a typical journal entry reads, "Party and horses much fatigued."[9] Finally, because everyone was bordering on starvation, Clark pushed ahead with six unnamed hunters (York probably among them) to break out of the mountains, kill game, and send it back. Even today one of the most impenetrable of all wilderness areas, the Bitterroots left a lasting mark on the men's memories for having taxed them to the limit. Many months later, Lewis would write, "not any of us have yet forgotten our suffering in those mountains in September last, and I think it probable we never shall."[10]

On September 20, having descended into an open plain, Clark came to two Nez Perce villages, where he and his men were given food. After

Edgar S. Paxon's conception of Lewis and Clark crossing the Bitterroot Range. York, carrying a pack on his back and holding his rifle upright, is in the lower center of the picture. *Courtesy of Burlington Northern Railroad.*

sending a supply of dried salmon and camas roots back to Lewis and the others, who were just coming out of the mountains, Clark received the welcome news that from here they would be able to travel by water. But before the building of canoes could begin, almost every member of the reunited party became violently ill from the unfamiliar diet of dried fish and roots. Many of the men were so debilitated they could not stand up or mount their horses without help, and, using some of the quaint medical terminology of the time, Clark has "nearly all Complaining of their bowels, a heaviness at the Stomach & Lax."[11] Perhaps because they were too sick to write more than a few sentences, or perhaps because they had grown accustomed to the Indians' reaction to York, the journalists make no mention of him meeting the Nez Perces. Nez Perce tribal legends, on the other hand, say he was once more the object of great curiosity. According to them, some members of the tribe tried "to wash the black off his face," while others, thinking he had been scorched in a fire, asked, "What had burned him up?"[12] It is also said he was named *Tse-mook-tse-mook To-to-kean*, meaning a black Indian, and that the name became the Nez Perce word for a black person.[13]

The men recovered, five canoes were hollowed out by fire in the Indian fashion (instead of being hacked out by hand), and the horses were turned over to the Nez Perces, who promised to care for them until the expedition returned. Starting down the Clearwater River on October 7, the once more waterborne explorers entered the Snake River and shot dangerous rapids they would have portaged around "if the season was not so far advanced and time precious with us."[14] On October 16, they arrived at the river they had long been seeking, the Columbia, the mouth of which had been discovered by an American sea captain just thirteen years earlier. With the Columbia's current moving them along, they soon saw evidence of the trade being carried on between the Indians at the coast and sailing ships sent from the United States and Great Britain to barter for valuable sea otter skins. Coming to an Indian settlement that exchanged goods with the coastal tribes, they were shown "two scarlet and a blue cloth blankets, also a Salors Jacket," tangible proof the Pacific could not be far distant.[15]

By this time, York and the others had cultivated a new taste in food. Game being scarce and everyone having become bored with dried fish and roots, "all the Party," except for Clark, had learned to "relish the flesh of

The expedition portaging around Celilo Falls on the Columbia, as presented in a mural in the rotunda of Oregon's state capitol. A youthful York is seated at the extreme right. *Oregon Department of Transportation.*

the dogs," a number of which had been purchased from the natives along the route.[16] Also, all along the route they had taken from the Rockies to the Upper Columbia, York had been the talk of the Indian tribes. In fact, according to two letters written long ago in Oregon to Eva Emery Dye, the author of a novel about Lewis and Clark, they were still talking about him a century after the explorers had passed through. One letter, written in 1903, says the Indians "speak of a negro being in the crowd & they give him the name of *the ravens son* as he was so black & the first negro they ever seen."[17] The other letter, written in 1904, reports an old Indian telling of "squaws trying to wash the Black off the Negro servant."[18]

For more than fifty miles, as the Columbia cut through the Cascade Range and dropped swiftly toward the sea, all the water skills of Lewis and Clark and their men were put to the test. Plunging over falls and churning through gorges—"swelling, boiling & whorling in every direction"—the river not only demanded exhausting portages, but, at places where the canoes could not be carried, it dictated that some of the men who were able to swim risk their lives by staying aboard while the others walked around

Frederic Remington's *Lewis and Clark on the Columbia* lacks the research that went into most of Charles M. Russell's paintings of the expedition. Here Lewis and Clark wear Revolutionary War uniforms, and their canoes are made of birchbark in the Eastern fashion instead of being Western-style dugouts. *Denver Public Library, Western History Department.*

the hazards with the expedition's most precious supplies.[19] Because he could swim, York was probably one of those who rode the canoes through the treacherous passages, although the journals do not give their names. The only definite identification of him along this stretch of the river is when Clark, referring to a group of Indians spending the night in camp, wrote: "one man played on the violin which pleased them much my servent danced."[20] These particular Indians seem not to have been troublesome, but just as the Columbia changed as it approached the sea so did the nature of the natives who lived along it. Described by one historian as "debauched by the maritime trade," most of the tribes of the Lower Columbia were thievish, disagreeable, and not impressed by these white men who had come out of the east.[21] Nor do they appear to have been impressed by York. They had seen black men before; indeed, years earlier a black sailor had been murdered by Indians on the Oregon coast when he tried to recover a weapon they had stolen.[22] That in the case of Lewis and Clark no blood was shed was due in large part to their alertness. Sensing the latent hostility, they had the men keep their weapons ready.

From the first day of the expedition to the last, most of the journal entries are matter-of-fact, devoid of any display of emotion. But on November 7, with the worst part of the Columbia behind them, Clark wrote two short sentences exploding with elation:*"Ocian in view! O! the joy."*[23] As it turned out, he was premature, having mistaken the river's wide estuary for the open sea, yet to all intents and purposes their journey had come to an end. On the other hand, the dangers and discomforts were far from at an end, for during the next week a storm lashed them without letup as they hugged the river's steep northern shore. Drifting trees "nearly 200 feet long" almost crushed the canoes; rain soaked them to their bones; and trying to camp was unrelieved misery, with "our canoes at one place at the mercy of the waves, our baggage in another; and our selves and party Scattered on floating logs and Such dry Spots as can be found on the hill sides, and crivicies of the rocks."[24] Food ran short and when the weather cleared York helped replenish it by shooting "2 geese and 8 Brant," a welcome accomplishment at the time, although not nearly as significant as one taking place two days later.[25] Then, as part of a group led by Clark, he walked nineteen miles to see the ocean, where standing on the beach he became the first black man to have crossed the continent north of Mexico.

Late in November, York did something else no black man had ever done before. Finding little game on the north side of the Columbia, Lewis and Clark allowed the contingent to vote as to where winter quarters should be located, a concession boldly disregarding military custom. At the same time, an even more unheard-of concession was made by the captains—and the soldiers as well. Gathered there at the far end of the continent in the year 1805, they allowed York, a slave, to cast a vote.[26] Not only did this make him the first black American known to have participated in an election west of the Mississippi River, but his being given a voice in the councils of the expedition seems to signify that he had come to be accepted as an almost equal member of the group. Nevertheless, his near-equality, if such were the case, did not last beyond the expedition's return to civilization in 1806. Contrary to the widely held belief that upon their arrival back in St. Louis Clark granted York freedom as a reward for his services, this did not happen. Although all of Lewis and Clark's men were mustered out with double pay and 320 acres of land, York remained a slave for at least five more years.

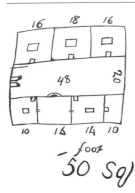

The floor plan of Fort Clatsop, drawn by Clark on the cover of a notebook bound in elk skin, shows the parade ground to have had rooms running along two sides. *From R. G. Thwaites, Original Journals of the Lewis and Clark Expedition.*

All except Private John Shields having voted to cross the river and examine the southern side, the party went there, found enough elk to provide badly needed food and clothing, and began to build Fort Clatsop. Named for the local tribe and located four or five miles from the ocean, it was a stockade fifty feet square enclosing a parade ground. When finished just before the year ended, this most distant of all American outposts had three rooms along one side and four opposite, all alive with fleas brought by the curious visiting Indians. During this period, York turns up in the journals more often than usual. He goes off to fish and shoot fowl with two men in a canoe, only to return empty-handed. He is sent with six men to bring in slain elk and is briefly lost. (Clark, who went to meet the group and waited half an hour for York to show up, says he "had stoped to rite his load and missed his way.")[27] Three times in December, Clark reports him sick—as were many of the others—and from one of these reports we learn that he helped construct the fort: "my boy york verry unwell from violent colds & strains carrying in meet and lifting logs on the huts to build them."[28] One sentence sounds as though York may have been given an unenviable chore while he was recovering. Clark reports taking "the precaution of haveing my blankets serched and the flees killed every day," and if, as he seems to say, he did not do this for himself, who else but York would have done it?[29]

On 1 January 1806, as the men celebrated the new year as best they could, Lewis looked ahead to 1 January 1807, "when in the bosom of our friends we hope to participate in the mirth and hilarity of the day, and when with the zest given by the recollection of the present, we shall completely, both mentally and corporally, enjoy the repast which the hand of civilization has prepared for us."[30] In less stilted words, he added that he hoped a year hence they would no longer be "eating our boiled Elk and wappetoe, and solacing our thirst with our only beverage *pure water*,"[31] To a man, the entire garrison at tiny, isolated, rain-sodden Fort Clatsop would have heartily agreed.

4. The Journey Home

Snow and frigid temperatures had been the hallmark of winter back at Fort Mandan; here it was endless rain. Sergeant Gass, who was fond of statistics, noted that from November 4 until March 25 "there were not more than twelve days in which it did not rain, and of these but six were clear."[1] The monotony of the rain was matched only by the monotony of the food: elk, a few deer, fish, roots, an occasional dog, and some whale blubber purchased from the Indians. Moreover, all the food had to be eaten without salt until a small seaside camp was established to boil it down from the ocean's water. Capitalizing on the monotony, the Indians brought their women to market "for a fishinghook or a stran of beads," resulting in a number of cases of venereal disease until Lewis made the men promise to have nothing more to do with them.[2] Although the neighboring Clatsops and the Chinooks from across the river were unaggressive, they were annoying. They would pilfer anything they could lay their hands on and drove the captains to distraction as "great higlers in trade," at one moment making outrageous demands for an article and at the next capriciously accepting much less for it.[3] By and large, Lewis and Clark liked these Indians—as they did most of the other tribes they had met this far—but both men had served with the army on the frontier and knew that vigilance could never be relaxed. Sentries were posted day and night, and at sunset Fort Clatsop's gate was closed.

The journals shed little light on how York spent the winter. He very likely went out with the hunters who had to range farther and farther from the fort to find elk; as did the other men, he undoubtedly made new moccasins and buckskins for the homeward journey; and, if the pattern of him usually being close to his master held true, he was one of a largely unnamed group Clark took to see the carcass of a whale which had washed ashore. He also must have been nearby as the captains spent long hours on paperwork, ex-

John Clymer's *Visitors at Fort Clatsop*. The local tribes who visited and traded with the explorers at their Pacific outpost were friendly, but Lewis and Clark nevertheless ordered the fort's gate to be closed every night. *Courtesy of John Clymer.*

panding and codifying the observations they had made to date of flora, fauna, Indian ways, and, particularly in the case of Clark, the geography of the country west of the Mandan villages. During this time, Lewis and Clark expressed the wish that a sailing ship would enter the Columbia so they could stock up on trade goods needed to deal with the Indians on the return journey, their supply by now having been reduced to a pittance. What no one knew is that the *Lydia* out of Boston had come into the harbor shortly after they had arrived back in November, but for some inexplicable reason the local tribes had not told them of it.[4]

On March 7, with spring approaching, Lewis wrote, "a bird of a scarlet colour as large as a common pheasant with a long tail has returned, one of them was seen today near the fort by Cap[t] Clark's black man, I could not obtain a view of it myself."[5] As innocent as this sentence sounds, it is a good example of the way some writers in later years took similar entries and made far-fetched interpretations of their meaning. One used these words to support his assertion that York was a fabricator of stories not to be believed, while two others seem to have drawn upon the very same words to justify their equally unfounded claims that he was an accomplished naturalist.[6] In this instance, York came off better than usual, for more often than not the far-fetched things that have been written about him have been unflattering.

As the time of departure for home neared, Lewis and Clark took a precaution revealing they were not completely confident the expedition would get there. They gave some of the local Indians sheets of paper on which they had listed the names of the members of the party (including "York, a black man of Captain Clark's") and on which they had also written that they "who were sent out by the government of the U'States in May 1804. to explore the interior of the Continent of North America, did penetrate the same by way of the Missouri and Columbia rivers, to the discharge of the latter into the Pacific Ocean"—in other words, an affidavit testifying to the success of the exploration.[7] Realizing that a catastrophe could wipe out their entire group on the way home, they left these papers with the natives in the hope that at least one copy would find its way to civilization aboard a trading ship. By this means, the world would be informed of what they had done and the American claim to the Northwest would be strengthened. On March 23, having made a gift of their little fort to a friendly Clatsop chief named Comowool, the two captains, their twenty-nine men, Sacagawea, little "Pomp," and Scannon began the long-awaited journey.

Lewis and Clark were wise to leave the papers behind, for the Indians along the Lower Columbia were so surly Lewis became convinced that only the expedition's size "prevents their attempting to murder us."[8] York had the opportunity to witness this hostile attitude at close hand when he went with Clark and a few others to explore the Willamette River. Stopping at a village whose inhabitants sulked and refused to sell them food, they seem to have been on the edge of an unpleasant situation until Clark frightened the Indians by magically moving the needle of his compass with a magnet and throwing a short length of an artillery fuse into a fire, causing the flames to change color. Farther upriver the mood of the Indians improved, as did Lewis and Clark's means of transportation. Gradually dispensing with the canoes that could move only slowly against the Columbia's current, they purchased more and more horses from the increasingly friendly tribes along the way. Finally, by the time they left the especially hospitable Wallawallas, they had enough horses to travel rapid-

The compass Clark carried on the expedition. By using a magnet to move its needle, he intimidated some unfriendly Indians along the Willamette River. *Smithsonian Institution.*

ly overland and rejoin the Nez Perces in May. There they received disheartening news: the snow was so deep in the Rockies a crossing would not be possible until the beginning of June at the earliest.

To the disappointment of all, the trail over the Bitterroots remained closed until late in June. As they waited impatiently, the journalists repeatedly referred to the expedition's need for food. With game seldom to be found and salmon not yet running in the river, the Nez Perces themselves were subsisting mainly on bread made from the roots of the camas plant, which although plentiful the captains would not let the men gather for themselves because of its resemblance to poisonous hemlock. Trade goods being so few that some other way was needed to obtain food, Clark now resorted to the practice of medicine and accepted roots for his fees. While with the tribe the previous autumn, he had brought about what to the Nez Perces was a miraculous cure by giving a man liniment to rub on his aching knee, and now patients flocked to him with complaints of sore eyes, abcesses, rheumatism, and even paralysis, all of which were treated with medicines Lewis and Clark knew were harmless.

Frankly admitting that they were engaging in a bit of quackery, Lewis was amused to find "my friend Capt. C. is their favorite phisician" and at the same time grateful for the food he brought in.[9] But Lewis himself could not refrain for long from practicing medicine, volunteering his diagnosis of some of the men's sickness as due to the camas. "Frazer, J. Fields and Wiser complain of violent pains in their heads," he wrote, "and Howard and York are afflicted with the colic. I attribute these complaints to their diet of roots [to] which they have not been accustomed."[10] Bored with their enforced wait and the dreary root menu—relieved only occasionally with the meat of a horse, a dog, or a deer—all became more and more anxious to move on to the plains of the Upper Missouri, where they knew game abounded. At last, when the captains felt they would shortly be able to leave, they parceled out the last of the precious trade goods among the men with instructions to try to barter for enough roots to survive the crossing of the mountains. While the journals do not say whether York had served as an assistant in Clark's makeshift clinic, they tell us he was now given the responsibility of trading for food.

From their terrible earlier experience in the Bitterroots, everyone knew how important it was to obtain as many roots as possible with the few remaining trade items. It therefore testifies to Lewis and Clark's trust in York's judgment that they allowed him to do some trading for their own needs. He first was sent with the interpreter Toussaint Charbonneau and Jean Baptiste Lepage to a village across the Clearwater River, where they spent the night and returned in the morning with four bags of roots and some camas bread. A few days later, their trade goods completely exhausted, the captains cut the buttons off their coats, added some eyewash and empty containers from their medical supplies, and sent him out again, this time with Hugh McNeal. Lewis's journal entry reflects his delight with the transaction they made: "in the evening they returned with about 3 bushels of roots and some bread having made a successfull voyage, not much less pleasing to us than the return of a good cargo to an East India Merchant."[11]

In their journal entries for June 9, both Lewis and Clark observed that the Clearwater River had been falling for several days, a sign they interpreted to mean most of the snow had melted in the high country. Eager to resume the journey and hopeful the trail would open up at any moment, they moved the expedition's camp closer to the mountains. On June 17, a long file of horses carrying riders and piled high with packs began the steep ascent, but the Bitterroots once more proved to be formidable. Soon finding themselves "invelloped in snow from 12 to 15 feet deep" and realizing they would need guides to lead them over the barely discernible trail, Lewis and Clark ordered the first "retrograde march" since the expedition had been in the field.[12] Falling back to their last campground, they recruited several Nez Perce guides, and on June 24 they again headed up into the dark, brooding mountains they had come to dread.

This time they succeeded; in fact, they moved faster over packed snow covering rocks and fallen timber than they had been able to do back in September. Just six days later, they dropped down into a sheltered area they had previously named "*Travellers rest,*" where the men took it easy for a few days before Lewis and Clark put into effect a plan they had conceived while still at Fort Clatsop.[13] The details of the plan called for the expedition to be

Edgar S. Paxon's mural of Lewis and Clark's camp at Lolo Creek. They called the camp Traveler's Rest and stopped at it on both the outward and return journeys. York stands in the center of the picture, slightly behind Lewis, who is conversing with a Nez Perce. *Courtesy of Missoula County and the Missoula County Board of Trustees for Museums.*

divided temporarily into a number of smaller units, but in essence it meant that Lewis and a few men would ride overland and explore north along the Marias River while Clark with a larger number went to the Yellowstone River and explored it down to the Missouri. Agreeing to meet at the mouth of the Yellowstone, Lewis took leave of his friend "with much concern on this occasion although I hoped this seperation was only momentary."[14] Lewis's concern proved to be well-founded. Before they met again, his and his men's lives would be in danger, one Blackfoot brave would be dead, and another grievously wounded.

York went with Clark as usual, so he did not take part in the incident, although he certainly heard about it firsthand when Lewis and his men later told their story. Taking a shortcut to the Great Falls of the Missouri, where Sergeant Gass and five men were left to prepare for the return portage, Lewis, George Drouillard, and the two Field brothers headed for the Marias. Nine days later, in the vicinity of present-day Cut Bank, Montana, they met eight warriors of the Blackfoot tribe moving cross-country

Olaf Seltzer's *Lewis on the Marias—July 27, 1806* depicts a tense moment in the fight Lewis and his three men had with the Blackfeet. The Indian who was stabbed to death in the incident was the first Blackfoot ever killed by an American, and his death is said to have caused bitter enmity toward the Americans who came later. *The Thomas Gilcrease Institute of American History and Art, Tulsa, Oklahoma.*

with a herd of horses, and, despite being suspicious of each other, the two groups spent the night together. Lewis took the first watch, turned it over to Joseph Field with orders to call him if any of the Blackfeet attempted to leave camp, then went to sleep. At daybreak, when Field carelessly laid down his rifle, an Indian seized both it and the rifle of his sleeping brother. At the same time, two other Indians seized the rifles of the sleeping Lewis and Drouillard, both of whom awakened instantly and leaped to their feet. What followed was a fierce melee in which Reuben Field stabbed an Indian in the heart —"the fellow ran about 15 steps and fell dead"—and Lewis, having recovered his rifle, shot another in the stomach.[15] At this point, the remaining Indians fled, and not much later so did Lewis and his men. Fearing that many vengeful Blackfeet would soon come looking for them, they mounted their horses and rode all that day and much of the following night, finally reaching the Missouri above the mouth of the Marias in the morning. There, by extraordinary good luck, they met the portage party (now augmented by ten men sent to the Great Falls by Clark) coming down the river. Wasting no time, they boarded the boats and quickly put the danger of any pursuing Blackfeet behind them.

Clark and his party's trip to and down the Yellowstone was much less eventful. Crossing to the headwaters of the Jefferson River, they picked up the canoes and a cache of supplies left behind the year before, then proceeded by boat and on horseback to the Three Forks of the Missouri. There Sergeant Ordway and nine men were detached to take the canoes to the Great Falls, make the portage with Sergeant Gass's unit, and accompany them to rendezvous with Lewis at the mouth of the Marias. Clark with York and eleven others rode on to the Yellowstone River and descended along its banks for some distance until trees of a sufficient size were found to build two canoes. Here Sergeant Pryor and three men were dispatched to take the horses and a letter across country to the Mandan villages, but they never made it. When two nights later Indians who were probably members of the Crow tribe stole all their horses, Pryor and his men walked back to the Yellowstone, ingeniously constructed two small boats with buffalo skins, and eventually caught up with Clark on the Missouri.

During the time Lewis and Clark were separated, Clark's journal mentions York five times. We are told he killed an elk, showed his master "a

John Clymer's *Arrival of Sergeant Pryor.* While on the Yellowstone, Clark dispatched Pryor and three men to travel overland with a letter to the Mandan villages. Indians stole their horses, so they built bull boats (small, round boats made with buffalo skins) and eventually caught up with Clark's group on the Missouri. York stands by the campfire, as does Sacagawea with her child. *Courtesy of John Clymer.*

Tobaco worm" (why Clark thought this worthy of comment is unexplained), and, providing a small insight into what his body servant had come to relish as a delicacy, "killed a Buffalow Bull, as he informed me for his tongue and marrow bones."[16] More significantly, we are told that Clark named a small tributary of the Yellowstone "Yorks dry river," making this the second time he had named a geographical feature for his slave.[17] The last entry to take note of York in any of the journals was written by Clark on August 3. Having arrived at the mouth of the Yellowstone, he reported that for 636 miles he had floated down that river "in 2 Small Canoes lashed together in which I had the following Persons. John Shields, George Gibson, William Bratten, W. Labeech, Tous[t] Shabono his wife & child & my man York."[18]

Because mosquitoes were thick and game scarce at the mouth of the Yellowstone, Clark continued down the Missouri, finally joining forces

On 5 November 1806, a Boston news-paper printed this earlier report from Baltimore announcing "the arrival of Captains Lewis and Clark, from their expedition into the interior." One sentence reads: "They have kept an ample journal of their tour; which will be published, and must afford much intelligence." *Newspaper Collection, The New York Public Library, Astor, Lenox and Tilden Foundations.*

By the last Mails.

MARYLAND.   BALTIMORE, OCT. 29, 1806.

A LETTER from *St. Louis* (*Upper Louisiana*), dated *Sept.* 23, 1806, announces the arrival of Captains LEWIS and CLARK, from their expedition into the interior.—They went to the *Pacific Ocean ;* have brought some of the natives and curiosities of the countries through which they passed, and only lost one man. They left the *Pacific Ocean* 23d March, 1806, where they arrived in November, 1805 ;—and where some American vessels had been just before.—They state the Indians to be as numerous on the *Columbia* river, which empties into the *Pacific*, as the whites in any part of the U. S. They brought a family of the Mandan indians with them. The winter was very mild on the *Pacific*.—They have kept an ample journal of their tour ; which will be published, and must afford much intelligence.

with Lewis on August 12. When the two parties met, Clark was shocked to find that his friend and partner had been shot through the left thigh in a hunting accident. Dressed in leather, Lewis had been mistaken for an elk by the one-eyed Pierre Cruzatte, and although he was now in pain he would recover fully in a matter of weeks. With the assistance of the wind, the current, and the oars, the explorers moved rapidly to the Mandan villages, where they discovered that during their absence the fort they had wintered in the year before had been largely destroyed by fire. But it did not matter, for their mission had been accomplished and they were homeward bound.

After persuading a Mandan chief named Sheheke to accompany them to Washington, granting John Colter permission to return upriver with two trappers who had ventured this far in search of beaver pelts, and saying farewell to Charbonneau, Sacagawea, and little "Pomp," the two captains and their men were once more on their way.[19] The rushing waters of the Missouri swept them past river traders who were astonished to find them still alive; past Sergeant Floyd's grave, which they stopped to visit; past small outlying settlements that had not been there on their outward journey; and, finally, about noon on 23 September 1806, into St. Louis. Clark's businesslike account of their arrival does not begin to describe the excitement of the moment. He merely says: "we Suffered the party to fire off their pieces as a Salute to the Town. we were met by all the village and received a harty welcom from it's inhabitants &c."[20]

A great American odyssey had come to an end. For his part, York had seen the enormous size and variety of the American West, had been the first member of his race to cross it, and had helped make the crossing possible. Initially, his contributions seem to have been appreciated. According to one description of the warm reception the explorers were given in St. Louis, "Even the negro York, who was the body-servant of Clark, despite his ebony complexion, was looked upon with decided partiality, and received his share of adulation."[21] But the adulation did not last long. He soon returned to the obscurity of slavery and was forgotten—so completely forgotten that most Americans, black and white, have never even heard of him.

Display of some of the journals that were kept throughout the expedition at the insistence of President Jefferson. They leave no doubt York performed his share of the labors and duties required of every member of the party. *American Philosophical Society.*

5. York's Contributions Reappraised

While it is regrettable that most people have never heard of York, it is deplorable that the relatively few who have read something about him have in all likelihood been led to believe he was a buffoon. This is because in much of what has been written about Lewis and Clark he has been treated as a racial stereotype, a ludicrous figure not to be taken seriously and certainly one not to be thought of as having contributed to the exploration in any significant way. To illustrate how effectively prejudice has denied him the recognition he deserves, it is almost certain that if an opera is ever written about the expedition, Sacagawea will be the prima donna and he will only carry a spear. At least this is the way they have been cast to date, with Sacagawea receiving "what in the United States counts as canonization if not deification" for her role in the enterprise, whereas York has been relegated to the background.[1] This is by no means to detract from the Indian girl, who was helpful in a number of ways, but rather to point out how the myth-makers have either ignored or distorted the words of the original sources in order to glorify one while more often than not making the other the butt of biased humor.

The denigration of York began toward the end of the 1800s, a time when it was a common literary practice to portray blacks as comic characters—good-natured but irresponsible "darkies" who broke into song and dance at the drop of a hat, spoke with an improbably thick accent, shook and shivered at the thought of ghosts, and all the rest of the familiar clichés. Two authors in particular cut the die from which so many one-dimensional Yorks have since been stamped out. In 1893, when Elliott Coues edited a reissue of Nicholas Biddle's narrative version of the journals, he described York as a man with a "glib tongue" who liked to get drunk and brag about himself.[2] Then, not content to leave it at that, Coues belittled his role in the exploration. Striving to be humorous, he was nonetheless disparaging when he wrote, "York's stories grew with every glass that went down, till Mr. Biddle might have wondered what his History of the Expedition had to do with that multitudinous host who conquered the land, under the leadership of a black drum-major about ten feet tall."[3] Although Coues cited no sources of any kind for his allegations that York drank too much and brashly boasted that he had led the expedition, the source of his derisive metaphor, "black drum-major," is all too obvious. The subtle poison of prejudice had begun to flow, and for decades to come others would freely write things about York they would never have dreamed of writing about his white companions.[4]

In 1904, Eva Emery Dye called Sacagawea to national attention by resurrecting her from the largely forgotten past and making her the heroine of *The Conquest*, a novel about Lewis and Clark. Subtitled *The True Story of Lewis and Clark*, the book was industriously researched (the author wrote to the known descendants of every member of the expedition), but it was a novel just the same.[5] Although Mrs. Dye was not nearly as hard on York as Elliott Coues had been, she still made him a stock figure who grinned "until every ivory tooth glistened," loved to take his rifle and "slew dem buffaloes," and was so touchingly devoted to his master that he voluntarily stayed on as Clark's bodyguard after he was freed because, as he is made to say, "For sho'! who cud tek cah o' Mars Clahk so well as old Yawk?"[6] Mrs. Dye's treatment of York was not purposely malicious, only a reflection of the time in which she wrote. She was, however, a better novelist than historian, and she planted seeds that bore false fruit. In some instances embellishing the facts she had gathered, in others creating new Lewis and Clark folklore where none had existed before, she set in motion a number of myths which have persisted to this day. Not the least of them is that York, although always willing and cheerful, was little more than a lackey whose contributions to the expedition did not extend beyond waiting on his master.

Putting aside for the moment the many misrepresentations of York which followed in the wake of Elliott Coues and Eva Emery Dye, the York of the Lewis and Clark journals stands on his own. A close reading of those basic documents reveals that he did indeed play a meaningful role, if for no other reason than that he carried his share of the daily duties and labors required to advance the expedition along its course. This by itself was no small contribution and should have earned him the same degree of recognition given his companions, the rank and file who collectively have been honored for leading the way into the American West. But York's contributions do not end there. By his very presence he was of value to Lewis and Clark in their dealings with a number of Indian tribes, and, at the critical moment when Lewis met the Shoshonis, he was a factor—perhaps even the decisive factor—in making it possible for them to obtain horses and continue on.

The journals strongly suggest that York's blackness served the expedition as a passport to western tribes who were so curious to see such a strange creature, and so impressed after they had, they greeted the white visitors more cordially than they might otherwise have done. While it goes without saying that the white man's domination of the Indians was primarily due to his advanced weapons, he often reminded them of his superiority by displaying mysterious scientific instruments or by performing tricks with such simple gadgets as mirrors and magnets. These the astonished Indians called "big medicine," meaning something they could

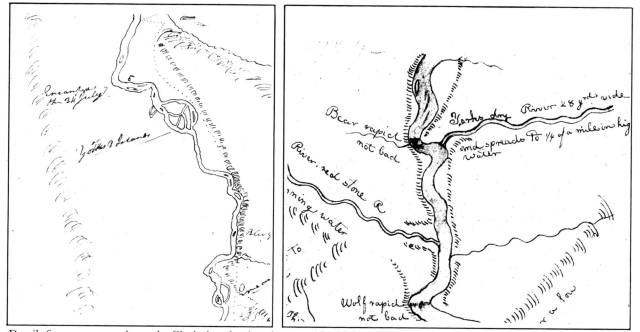

Details from two maps drawn by Clark show landmarks named for his body servant. On left, "Yorks 8 Islands" on the Upper Missouri. On right, "Yorks dry river" on the Yellowstone. *Left map from Western Americana Collection, the Beinecke Rare Book and Manuscript Library, Yale University; right map from the InterNorth Art Foundation, Joslyn Art Museum, Omaha, Nebraska.*

not comprehend and therefore viewed with awe as sacred, and part of this awe was in turn transferred to those who controlled the magic.[7] Of all the wonders Lewis and Clark paraded before tribes who had never seen a black man, none was more wonderful than York, as is testified to by Pierre Antoine Tabeau, a Missouri River trader who was with the Arikaras when the expedition arrived. Providing one of the rare physical descriptions of York written by anyone who saw him in the flesh, Tabeau observed: "The quadrant, phosphorus, and the magnet were regarded at the Captains' as medicine; that is to say, as supernatural and powerful. The most marvelous was, though, a large, fine man, black as a bear, who spoke and acted as one."[8] (The reference to York speaking and acting like a bear has to do with him telling the Arikaras he had been wild until caught and tamed by Clark.)

Time and again, the color of York's skin impressed the Indians, and at one point may even have intimidated them. A Nez Perce legend has it that when the hungry and weakened expedition came out of the Bitterroots, most of the tribe wanted to kill the white intruders, but were frightened of the black man who was with them. One version of the story describes the tribe's reaction in these words: "He had shining eyes that rolled around in his head. 'If we kill these others,' they said, 'the black man will surely kill us.' So they let the strangers come on."[9] Whether or not this legend has been enlarged and embroidered over the years (as is often the case with legends), it is true a number of tribes were awed by York's singularity, and it is also true he was the main attraction in Lewis and Clark's traveling magic show. While descending the Columbia, Clark gave Sacagawea's presence credit for having signaled the potentially hostile natives along the way that the expedition's intentions were peaceful, "as no woman ever accompanies a war party of Indians in this quarter."[10] Perhaps he and others since should have given York a little credit for also having smoothed the path.

Lewis and Clark were resourceful men, to say the least, so one cannot declare with absolute finality that they would not have found some way to cross the Rockies if they had failed to acquire horses from the Shoshonis. The odds against them having done it on foot, however, are enormous, because even with horses they barely survived the Bitterroots. Perhaps they would have gone back to the Mandan villages and tried to make contact with the Shoshonis or another horse-owning tribe the following year; perhaps they would have attempted to winter somewhere between the Mandans and the mountains (although at what cost cannot even be imagined); or perhaps, as Lewis feared and most likely would have happened, the lack of horses would have so discouraged the men "as to defeat the expedition altogether."[11] But this is an unknown. What is known is that while Lewis did all he could to keep the suspicious Shoshonis from running off with their horses before Clark and the main party could come up with the trade goods, he was not in control of the situation. As he was acutely aware, the fate of the expedition depended "in a great measure upon the caprice of a few savages who are ever as fickle as the wind."[12]

Fortunately for Lewis and Clark, those fickle savages were greatly intrigued at the thought of seeing a man with black skin. In fact, they were so eager to see him that, depending upon Lewis's and Biddle's varying accounts, they either rated him equal to or more important than the trade goods. Because the accounts differ slightly, it would be going too far to maintain that the news of York alone kept the Shoshonis in place. But, beyond any shadow of a doubt, he was one of the two most compelling reasons they did not vanish with their horses, leaving Lewis and Clark unable to go on. That York was the right person in the right place at the right time was, of course, not of his doing, so he cannot be credited with having consciously altered the outcome of the expedition. Still, in other instances where people made a difference simply by having been in the right place at the right time, history has not always been as forgetful as it has been of him.

Solely on the basis of what is written in the journals, there is reason to believe that York conducted himself in such a manner as to gain the esteem of his comrades as time went on. To recap some of the things he did which must have impressed them favorably, he was kind to Sergeant Floyd in his last hours; he regularly brought in welcome meat and fowl; he participated in the important reconnaissance of the Marias River; he continued to search for Clark and the Charbonneaus during the height of the fierce storm at the Great Falls; he went ahead with Clark and just two others to find the Shoshonis when it was not known whether they would be friendly or hostile; and his success in trading with the Nez Perces for badly needed food for the return crossing of the Bitterroots was applauded by Lewis himself. Moreover, because one of the journalists would have said so if York had conducted himself otherwise, it can be taken for granted he did everything that was asked of him, did not shrink from the hardships and the dangers, and served Lewis and Clark as faithfully as any of the other men. Perhaps most meaningful of all, when the location of winter quarters was being decided at the Pacific, his captains and his comrades waived all accepted practices and allowed him, a slave, to vote. Surely, this is not the profile of a man who, as so many writers would have us believe, was little more than a buffoon.

II

THE YORK OF MYTH
AND OF FACT

6. York as a Buffoon

In no fewer than nine books published between 1902 and 1958—a significant percentage of all the books having something to do with Lewis and Clark that appeared during those years—the York of the expedition's journals was distorted beyond all recognition.[1] Although six of the books were novels and therefore not to be judged as history, they nevertheless indelibly imprinted on the minds of unknowing readers an impression of York as a black buffoon whose only contribution to the undertaking was to make his companions laugh. The other three books, all purporting to be serious nonfiction, also contain unflattering and racially-related references to him, and one of them (ostensibly a biography of Meriwether Lewis) is in a class by itself as the most irresponsible work ever published about the exploration.[2] If any doubt exists that much of what has been written about York is tainted with prejudice, a glance at what these books have to say quickly dispels it.

Emerson Hough, in his novel *The Magnificent Adventure*, has Clark telling Lewis he will take York on the expedition because "a negro is always good-natured under hardship, and a laugh now and then will not hurt any of us."[3] Donald Culross Peattie, in his novel *Forward the Nation*, has York sending his companions into stitches with his fear of bears when he accounts for the absence of Indians at one point in the journey by saying, "They skeered plum out o' heah by the b'ars, like me."[4] In the category of nonfiction, Charles Wilson, author of *Meriwether Lewis of Lewis and Clark* (the prizewinner for irresponsibility cited above), describes York as "bullet-headed, ivory-toothed" and flashing "a smile to be measured with a foot rule," although he does not reveal how he came by this information.[5] Nor does Wilson share the secret of how he made this extraordinary discovery: "The fact that he was double-jointed at the knees and ankles helped mightily with his prowess at jigging and pigeon-wing cutting."[6]

In two other works of nonfiction, the authors completely ignore what the journals report and equate York with Scannon, the big Newfoundland, as the only members of the expedition who in the early stages of the journey "could be depended upon to do what they were instructed to do."[7] Not only does this as much as say he was as obedient as a dog while Lewis and Clark's other men were insubordinate, which is ridiculous, but it also carries with it the implication that York was a Negro who, as the expression goes, "knew his place." In short, all nine of the books published between 1902 and 1958 in one way or another present York as a caricature, a happy-go-lucky behemoth of a man who plays the fool with "eye-rolling abandon," attires himself garishly in "an outfit of baggy blue denim cloth, tied at the middle with a blood-red sash," leers at the Indian girls with "lecherous joy," and reassures Julia Hancock, Clark's bride-to-be, that he will share the perils of the wilderness with his master because "Marse Billy couldn't go off nohow on no such trip like dat widout ole Yawk goin' along."[8]

From these and similar absurdities the York of myth was born, a creation of prejudice masquerading as history. Little more need be said about such blatantly biased writing than that it was an unfortunate product of the past and unfounded on any sources whatever. While the journals tell us that York danced (as did the other men, for it was one of their few amusements), they give no details of how he danced, and they definitely do not justify one historian's offhand remark that he performed "Negro dances."[9] Despite what others have written, the journals themselves are silent as to the whiteness of York's teeth, the shape of his head, his attire when not wearing buckskins, the thickness of his accent, the way he looked at the Indian girls, and whether or not he was more afraid of bears than any man in his right senses should be. When the two are compared, the York of the journals and the York of Lewis and Clark folklore are startlingly different people. One is a man who shouldered his share of the duties and hardships of the expedition to the satisfaction of his captains and his comrades. The other steps right out of a minstrel show.

While York was certainly no buffoon, it is only natural to wonder whether he had a sense of humor. According to two respected Lewis and Clark scholars, he did. In fact, they say he was a fun-filled man who lifted the spirits of his fellow members of the expedition with his jokes and playful antics. Richard Dillon, author of a standard biography of Lewis, describes him as "a jolly giant of a fellow whose wit made a long and hard journey seem shorter to the men."[10] Along the same lines, Ernest Osgood, the editor of Clark's field notes, comments that "York undoubtedly furnished much amusement to the men, but was often a problem for his master," adding that on one occasion he had to be admonished for carrying a joke too far.[11] By no means a caricature, this York is an appealing figure, one of those lighthearted mavericks who often crop up in military units to relieve the moments of tension and the hours of boredom with laughter. One would like to think he was this way, for it would add a dimension to his personality and enhance his value as a member of the party. Unfortunately, however, there is little documentary support for Dillon's and Osgood's contentions. A search through the more than one million words contained in all the journals reveals only one instance when York played a prank and no instance when he was admonished by his master.

On 10 October 1804, while the expedition was still moving up the Missouri and had just met the Arikaras, Clark recorded a bizarre scene in his field notes for the day. He described York telling these Indians who had never seen a black man that he had once been wild and had lived as a cannibal by eating people. In Clark's words, the Arikaras "were much astonished at my black Servent, who, made him self more turrible in thier view than I wished him to Doe as I am told telling them that before I caught him he was wild & lived upon people, young children was verry good eating."[12] Clark's graphic picture of York frightening the Indians leaves no doubt he put on a convincing show, and it is not difficult to imagine his comrades doubled over with laughter. There can also be no doubt his performance was intended as a joke, for Clark's final journal entry says "he Carried on the joke" to the point where in Clark's opinion he carried it too far.[13] Where some doubt arises is as to whether the joke was York's idea.

Clark's remark that York made himself more terrible "than I wished him to Doe" could mean he had been given a part to play and had overacted it to his master's discomfiture, although even then no mention is made of him being admonished. At the very least, the words "than I wished him to Doe" imply that Clark knew about the joke in advance. But while it is conceivable the joke was Clark's or someone else's idea, several sources other than the journals suggest that it was probably York's after all. As will be seen, two accounts of him in St. Louis after the expedition have him regaling tavern audiences with preposterous tales along the lines of the one he told the Arikaras, and a source from within the Clark family describes him reciting "his adventures with dramatic pose."[14] It therefore seems that York actually did have a sense of humor and did enjoy telling a good story. Nevertheless, the fact remains that when Dillon and Osgood, with the best of intentions, characterized him as the source of constant amusement throughout the long exploration, they were reading more into the journals than is actually there.

The Arikaras were not afraid of York for long. As Sergeant Ordway wrote a few days after the wild-man episode: "the Greatest Curiousity to them was York Capt Clarks Black Man. all the nation made a great deal of him."[15] One of the reasons he was the focus of attention was, of course, his blackness. Another was his unusually large size. But there was still another reason why they "all flocked around him & examin^d him from top to toe."[16] His strength was so prodigious it also put him in the limelight, with Clark's words giving reason to believe that York was quick to show it off. The day before he pretended to have been a wild man, Clark wrote in his journal that York "did not lose the opportunity of [displaying] his powers Strength &c. &c.," and the next day, immediately after describing the performance York put on, Clark entered in his field notes that "he showed them his strength &c. &c."[17] If, as it appears, York relished the admiration lavished on him by the Indians, who can blame him? Indeed, if he had not, he would have been almost as superhuman as they thought he was.

For a slave to have been admired by anyone had to have been a most unusual and exhilarating experience. As the author of a major work on slavery has pointed out, one of the most effective methods by which new slaves were broken to bondage and succeeding generations trained was to instill in them "a consciousness of personal inferiority," a feeling that "their color was a badge of degradation."[18] Having come from a society where to be black was to be looked down upon by even the most ignorant of whites, the adulation accorded him by the Indians must have been very heady stuff, to say the least, and for him to have been indifferent to it would have been remarkable. At the same time, it would have been remarkable if in the privacy of his mind he had not drawn disturbing comparisons between his treatment by the so-called savages and the treatment of most slaves by those who considered themselves civilized and the Indians heathens in need of missionaries to save their souls.

Charles M. Russell's *York in the Camp of the Mandans*. Indians who had never seen a black man viewed York with astonishment and awe as an almost supernatural being—in their words, "big medicine." One chief, not believing his skin could possibly be black, spit on his finger and tried to rub off the paint. *Gift of C. M. Russell, Montana Historical Society.*

John Clymer's *Up the Jefferson*. While Lewis and three men went ahead in search of the Shoshonis, whose horses the expedition needed to cross the Rockies, Clark led the main party with the dugout canoes up the Jefferson River. Sacagawea walks just ahead of York. *Courtesy of John Clymer.*

Charles M. Russell's *Lewis and Clark on the Lower Columbia*. Sacagawea interprets as Clark holding a rifle and York holding a paddle look on. Although thought by some to depict the expedition's arrival at Gray's Bay in 1805, it is more likely the painting is set at the time the explorers started home in 1806. During the winter they spent at the mouth of the Columbia, they obtained two carved and decorated Indian canoes like the ones shown here. *Courtesy Amon Carter Museum, Fort Worth*.

John Clymer's *Buffalow Gangue*. While floating down the Yellowstone on the journey home, Clark wrote that his party was forced to land because a large "gangue of buffalow" was crossing the river. York, who can be seen with his rifle ready, is frequently cited in the expedition's journals for shooting game. *Courtesy of John Clymer.*

7. York and the Indian Women

A number of authors who have written about York's amorous adventures while he was in the West have simultaneously disapproved of and been fascinated by the thought of a black man having sexual relations with women not of his own race. At the same time they have frowned on his involvement with the Indian women for having made him "a horrible nuisance" to Lewis and Clark, they have dwelled at length upon his triumphs as "a black conqueror leaving behind his copper-skinned captives," a man tribe after tribe showered with feminine "favors," and one who "took full advantage of his popularity" while most of his white companions virtuously "withstood the temptation well."[1] By maximizing York's sexual prowess and minimizing the part he played in the expedition, these writers unwittingly demonstrated the validity of an observation made by two psychiatrists about a neither new nor uncommon white view of blacks. Reflecting upon the dichotomy with which black males are often perceived, they wrote: "The black man occupies a very special sexual role in American society. He is seen as the ultimate in virility and masculine vigor. But at the same time he is regarded as socially, economically, and politically castrated, and he is gravely handicapped in performing every other masculine role."[2]

In *Tale of Valor*, a novel published as recently as 1958, Vardis Fisher pulled out all the stops in magnifying York's virility to the point where he is bluntly called "the black bull."[3] Of the forty-eight pages on which Fisher mentions York, twenty-nine are devoted to dialogue and descriptive passages featuring his lewd behavior, Clark's disgust with that behavior, and the resentment, tinged with envy, of his white companions. As a sample of Fisher's absorption with this theme, York's "easy conquest of the red women" makes him arrogant; when the party leaves the Mandans and their women, Reuben Field says with disdain, "That's the nigger's last chance before the Blackfeet scalp him"; and on the return journey more than a few tiny Yorks "with negroid features and kinky hair" are discovered among the tribes previously visited.[4] Obsessed with the subject, Fisher far outdistanced all other writers with his intemperate characterization of York as a cliché of black virility.[5] But *Tale of Valor* is a novel and its perpetuation of the age-old myth that blacks are more virile than whites is perhaps to be expected. What is unexpected is that two Lewis and Clark scholars seem to have been so influenced by the same myth they failed to take into account what the journals have to say about the matter.

In 1904, Olin Wheeler, author of *The Trail of Lewis and Clark*, wrote of York that "the tribes from the mouth of the Missouri to the mouth of the Columbia took particular pains to propitiate his sable majesty, and he was overwhelmed with feminine attentions."[6] In 1940, Elijah Criswell, author of *Lewis and Clark: Linguistic Pioneers*, made a similar all-encompassing remark when he stated, "Clark's black servant, York, even had his penis *frosted* a little, an unfortunate accident that may have diminished the embarrassing interest always shown by the Indian damsels in this popular son of Ham."[7] When Wheeler and Criswell took liberties with York by condescendingly calling him "his sable majesty," making a questionable joke about his case of frostbite, and finding it embarrassing for the Indians girls to have been enamored of a black man, they also took liberties with the sources. No document in which York is named supports their sweeping assertions to the effect that he was sought out and bedded down all along the expedition's route. In fact, the journals actually say less about him with regard to members of the opposite sex than they do about many of his white companions, a number of whom (York not among them) had to be treated for venereal disease.[8]

With so much having been written about York's sexual encounters, it comes as a surprise to find that nowhere in any of the journals kept while the expedition was in progress is any reference made to him and the Indian women. Only in the narrative version of the journals, written by Nicholas Biddle and published eight years after the expedition had been completed, are two short accounts to be found. One is the story about an Arikara husband guarding his lodge's entrance while York was with his wife, and the other is about "two very handsome young squaws," also Arikaras, who made themselves available to York and the others aboard the keelboat.[9] However, while it is true that these are the only recorded instances of York having had relations with Indian women, it would be naïve to think his liaisons ended there. Biddle as much as said they did not when he added this sentence to the story of the girls aboard the keelboat: "The black man York participated largely in these favors; for, instead of inspiring any prejudice, his color seemed to procure him additional advantage from the Indians, who desired to preserve among them some memorial of this wonderful stranger."[10] In other words, the Indians thought that by means of intercourse they could acquire and pass along in their bloodlines some of his "big medicine," a practice frequently observed by plains tribes when they came in contact with strangers possessing wealth or power they did not have. But even when it is granted that York had more than the two affairs reported by Biddle, this still does not explain the consuming preoccupation of so many writers with the subject, especially in view of the more numerous journal entries about the other men and Indian women. One can only wonder whether the subject would ever have come up if York had not been black.

The impression that York left a trail of progeny all along the expedition's path has become so engrained in Lewis and Clark folklore that Robert Penn Warren, the distinguished poet and novelist, was prompted to write:

> And my good nigger York, who left his seed
> In every tribe across the continent—[11]

While there is no intentional malice in Warren's words, there is more poetry than truth, just as there is more imagination than documentation behind equally unfounded statements along the lines of "the young bloods vied with one another to bring him their squaws."[12] Actually, there is no documentation of any kind to warrant the assumption that York increased the population of every Indian village he visited, and the little evidence indicating that he did father a few children is hearsay in nature.

An oral tradition among the Lemhi Shoshonis has it that York sired a son called *Too-tivo*, meaning a black white man.[13] Among the Nez Perces, a legend has been passed down saying that a child of mixed blood was born, but died before reaching maturity.[14] With respect to another Nez Perce legend, John Bakeless has written: "Like a good many of the other members of the expedition, York had a temporary Indian 'wife.' On the return journey, he found that he had become the father of a little Nez Percé Negro. Occasional modern Nez Percés with kinky hair are perhaps descended from this child."[15] Of the Mandans, a man who lived in North Dakota in 1899 maintained that signs of York could still be detected among them, but he raised doubts about his credibility by attributing the fair complexion of that tribe to the earlier presence of the Lewis and Clark party.[16] (From the first time white men met the Mandans, long before Lewis and Clark, they were impressed by their light skin.) Still another reference to York having fathered children is the most interesting of all, for it came from none other than William Clark.

On 13 September 1832, before taking a tour of the prairies, Washington Irving of "Rip Van Winkle" and "The Legend of Sleepy Hollow" fame visited Clark at his country home outside St. Louis, where in the course of the conversation York was discussed. Presumably at the time or later the same day, Irving made notes of the conversation which have turned out to be the single most important source of the knowledge there is of York's post-expedition years. Among other things, Clark told Irving he had freed York, had set him up in a drayage business that failed, and that he had died of cholera in Tennessee. He also referred in what appears to have been a humorous vein to his former slave having fathered children while on the expedition, with Irving's last note reading, "Some of the traders think they have met traces of York's crowd, on the Missouri."[17] From this one sentence, Biddle's two short passages, and a few Indian legends, a myth was spawned that York had a field day with Indian women clear across the West and left them with more than memories. It is ironic this happened, particularly since York is not the only one the Indians mention as having left offspring behind. Curiously, most writers have had nothing to say about another Indian legend naming Clark himself as the father of a Nez Perce son who had light hair, blue eyes, and in old age was taken prisoner during Chief Joseph's War.[18]

Perhaps those writers who placed so much emphasis on York's sexual activities felt more comfortable attributing licentiousness to a black man than to whites. Perhaps they largely ignored the womanizing of the other men because they could not bring themselves to admit that among the white explorers they presented to their readers as national heroes there were men with feet of clay. Or perhaps they automatically assumed that York was the delight of the native women simply because of the entrenched belief by whites that blacks are exceptionally virile. Whatever the reason, when the original sources are consulted, it quickly becomes clear that their stories about him were influenced less by the facts than by the color of his skin.

8. The York of the St. Louis Taverns

A recurring story about York is that he was freed shortly after the expedition returned, began to drink more than he should have, and became a flamboyant figure in the frontier town of St. Louis, known for colorfully embellishing his exploits while with Lewis and Clark. Of the three parts of the story, the first is false, the second is doubtful, and the third appears to be true. Contrary to long-standing Lewis and Clark tradition, York was not freed when the expedition returned in 1806, nor, for that matter, until a number of years had passed. He probably was not a heavy drinker, for in the conversation Clark had with Washington Irving in 1832, during which he commented on some of York's failings, he did not include drinking as one of them. On the other hand, if two reports derived from word-of-mouth accounts handed down in St. Louis from the early 1800s are to be believed, York had a flair for entertaining tavern audiences with tall tales which, in the words of one of those accounts, "would not have been discreditable to the imagination of the author of Baron Munchausen."[1]

York has at times been described either as a drunkard and braggart or more moderately as a tippler and spinner of yarns, depending upon the individual writer's point of view. In 1893, without citing any sources, Elliott Coues flatly declared that York "used to get drunk," then enlarged upon the point by saying his stories "grew with every glass that went down" until he featured himself as having been the leader of the expedition.[2] Other authors who also cited no sources seem to have picked up Coues's reference to drinking and passed it along until this image of an inebriated York found a niche in the literature about Lewis and Clark, with a fairly typical description reading, "By this time [just after the expedition] the tales that black York told, when he was liquored up, were long as Missouri and tall as the Rockies."[3] Finally, in 1970, a book ostensibly based upon thorough research gave this image renewed currency and credibility. In his *The Men of the Lewis and Clark Expedition*, Charles Clarke states that York "took to drink and entertained with stories about his adventures with the expedition, which became taller with each telling," adding in a footnote that he had obtained this and other information from documents in the possession of the Missouri Historical Society.[4] At last, someone had nailed down the facts about York. Or so it seemed. Upon investigation, however, it was found that the Missouri Historical Society is in possession of no such documents.[5]

When some writers cite no sources and another writer cites sources which do not exist, one is left to wonder how they came by their information. A natural first step in trying to trace the origins of statements made about York is to go back to Washington Irving's notes of his conversation with Clark and see if they say anything along the same lines. As it turns out, one note does, referring to York as "the hero of the Missouri expedition & adviser of the Indians," words unmistakably meaning that he had at some time exaggerated his role in the exploration.[6] Whether Clark mentioned this jocularly and without disapproval, as Irving's words seem to imply, there is now no way of knowing. There is also now no way of knowing whether York had played up his role seriously or with a wink, although it is all but inconceivable to think a slave would have been so brash as to make such a claim other than humorously. Nevertheless, while Irving's notes tell us York engaged in what sounds like humorous hyperbole, they could not possibly have been the source of Coues's remark that "he used to get drunk" and Clarke's remark that "he took to drink." Nowhere in any of the notes is anything said about him drinking, not even, as might be expected, as one of the several reasons Clark gave Irving for his later failure with a drayage business. For that matter, Irving's notes could not have been the source of Coues's statement about him claiming to have led the expedition, for the notes did not first appear in print until 1919, long after Coues had written.[7] Instead, what may have happened is that Coues drew upon—and greatly distorted—two little-known accounts of York which were passed down in St. Louis from the time of Lewis and Clark. But this is only a speculation, for Coues never troubled to document any of his derisive comments about the man he called "a black drum-major."

In 1860, in a book about the West that included early St. Louis lore, the authors described the return of the Lewis and Clark Expedition and the warm reception given the two captains and their men. Then, turning their attention to the only black member of the party, they wrote:

> Even the negro, York, who was the body-servant of Clark, despite his ebony complexion, was looked upon with decided partiality, and received his share of adulation. It is said that York was much given to romance, and under the excitement of frequent spirituous potations, with which his kind friends furnished him in abundance, would relate the most thrilling incidents which befell him and the party during the long voyages through the wilderness, and which would not have been discreditable to the imagination of the author of Baron Munchausen, when in his happiest flights of erratic fancy.[8]

An 1883 history of St. Louis related a similar story, although dating it at least a year after the expedition's return, when both Lewis and Clark were residents of that town:

> How it used to delight the boatmen, in the time of Governors Lewis and Clark, to get the latter's body-servant, York, into the taverns, ply him with liquor till the *miles gloriosus* rose within him to the Munchausen pitch, and then "draw him out," in order to make him out-brag the trappers and cap their marvelous stories with tales more marvelous still. They could not gainsay him neither, for he had been farther than they. He had followed his master across the great divide and down the Columbia River, until the camp was pitched within sight and sound of the long, murmurous rollers of the great Pacific Ocean.[9]

Because these two passages are based upon word-of-mouth traditions, they must be questioned. They were written long after the events they describe, and it is axiomatic that stories perpetuated orally are often altered in the telling and retelling. On the other hand, they go back closer to the time when York lived than do any other references to him frequenting the St. Louis taverns, and insofar as they portray him as a teller of tales in the mold of Baron von Münchhausen, they seem to be corroborated both by Washington Irving's note about him exaggerating and by Clark's earlier description of him telling the Arikaras he had been a wild man. Although it is impossible to say whether or not the picture they give of him is true to life, one wants to believe it. Unlike the minstrel-show stereotype so many writers have made him out to have been, this York of the candlelit taverns is appealingly human. He comes across as a man of warmth and humor; a man who enjoyed his drinks and his audience; a man who "despite his ebony complexion, was looked upon with decided partiality"; and a man who was adept at a skill highly admired along the frontier, that of spinning outlandish yarns. If nothing else, these passages written just before and not long after the Civil War are interesting in that when they are compared with much that would be written about him later—even well into the twentieth century—they are remarkably free of prejudice.

9. The Revisionists Discover York

Over the years, York's contributions to the Lewis and Clark Expedition have been largely ignored. In this regard, he fared much the same as did many generations of blacks whose contributions to all facets of American life since their forefathers had been brought here in chains were either played down or passed over. But then, as society became increasingly aware of racial wrongs and began to try to right them, a change took place. A surge of interest in black history led to many books and articles making the point that the white view of the past was almost exclusively one-sided, and solidly reinforcing the point with biographies of black men and women whose achievements had not previously been reported. Needless to say, this ongoing effort to set the record straight is essential if the diversity and richness of the nation's heritage is to be fully appreciated. On the other hand, it is unfortunate that at times this effort has led to abuses. Just as some earlier writers distorted facts for reasons rooted in prejudice, some relatively recent writers have distorted them out of an overly zealous desire to balance the scale. In the case of York, a few writers have already tried to make him something he never was.

In "York, the Slave Explorer," an article appearing in *Negro Digest* in 1962, K.D. Curtis seems to have been the first to present a York miraculously transformed. Suddenly, he became "one of the most important expedition members," invaluable to Lewis and Clark because he "spoke French and several Indian dialects," an accomplished naturalist who "discovered new wildlife species" in the West, and a man of fearless courage who climbed down into the flooding ravine at the Great Falls to rescue Clark, Sacagawea, and her child by using "his powerful physique as a human hoist."[1] The sources and justifications Curtis gives for these surprising statements are equally surprising. His version of the incident in the ravine, which bears no resemblance to how the journals tell it, is attributed to "an official Army account of Western-frontier action," whatever that may be, although it sounds like a new way of citing none other than the journals themselves.[2] He gives no source for his claim that York discovered new species of wildlife, but neither did the novelist Eva Emery Dye, from whom Curtis probably received the idea.[3] And while he also does not trouble to document York's ability to speak several Indian dialects, he justifies his statement that York spoke French on the grounds he picked it up during visits to St. Louis while the expedition wintered at Camp Wood across the Mississippi. If York did learn French at this time, he must have had a gift for languages bordering on genius. According to the journal Clark kept at Camp Wood, York went with him to St. Louis only once, and then for a visit of just six days. In short, Curtis's York is more than a man revised; he is a man reborn, so different from all previous accounts that even his mother would not have recognized him.

Following on Curtis's heels, William Katz, in *Eyewitness: The Negro in American History*, endows York with a body "well over six feet in height and 200 pounds in weight."[4] While the journals clearly say he was a very large man, Katz's description is nonetheless based on imagination, not on any eyewitness report, for in all the references made to York by those who knew him, none gives any statistics as to his size. Katz goes on to repeat the story that York was Lewis and Clark's indispensable interpreter of French, a misconception shared by many and apparently based upon a sentence written by Charles McKenzie, a North West Company trader who visited the Mandan villages from Canada while Lewis and Clark were there. Describing the slow and tedious process by which translations from Gros Ventre to English were made, McKenzie wrote, "A mulatto, who spoke bad French and worse English, served as interpreter to the Captains, so that a single word to be understood by the party required to pass from the Natives to the woman [Sacagawea], from the woman to the husband [Charbonneau], from the husband to the mulatto, from the mulatto to the captains."[5] Because no record of the expedition lists a mulatto among its members, and because Charbonneau was a French Canadian who could speak no English, a number of writers have seized upon this account of a Tower of Babel at the Mandans as proof that York spoke French.[6] McKenzie's sentence is puzzling, to say the least, with the identity of the mulatto still a mystery. But, whoever he was, the evidence is overwhelming that he was not York.

Two reliable sources assure us that York was not a mulatto, and Lewis himself makes it clear that he was not the expedition's interpreter of French. Far from being a mulatto—by definition either the offspring of a white parent and a black parent or a person of mixed ancestry with light-brown skin—York was the son of slaves and a man with very black skin. John Clark, William's father, stated in his will that York, "one Negroe man," was born of parents who were both slaves, and Pierre Antoine Tabeau, the trader with the Arikaras who saw York in person, described him as "black as a bear."[7] As for York speaking French, to believe this we would have to believe that a slave boy growing up in Virginia and Kentucky received French lessons when his master received none, a circumstance totally illogical in light of what is known about the education of slaves. However, it is not necessary to rely on logic to refute the assertion that he was depended upon to translate French. Lewis did this conclusively in a post-expedition letter to the secretary of war. Reviewing the various contributions of the men, he singled out Francis Labiche for having "rendered me very essential services as a French and English interpreter."[8]

The revised York has come a long way by the time he appears in Phillip Drotning's *An American Traveler's Guide to Black History,* a book commendably devoted to "the efforts of Negroes as Americans, in behalf of America."[9] As a member of the expedition, York did serve his country well—far better than is generally realized—but one must wonder how well both he and black history are served by such extravagant claims as "York spoke fluent Sioux" and acted as "guide" of the Lewis and Clark Expedition.[10] Regrettably, Drotning cites no source for York having mastered such a difficult language as Sioux while the expedition was only briefly with two branches of the tribe, nor does he explain why Lewis and Clark saw fit to enlist the temporary services of Sioux-speaking Pierre Dorion before they entered Sioux country. Drotning also offers no support for what may be the most astonishing of all claims ever made about York. To be told he was Lewis and Clark's guide makes the reader's jaw drop. How, one must wonder, was it possible for a slave who had never been out of the South to point the way across the West?

"Explorer with Lewis and Clark," an article appearing in a 1982 issue of the *Negro History Bulletin*, makes a mockery of the very thing it purports to be, a work of scholarship. Written by Nicholas Polos, a man identified as a professor of history at a university in California, the article is said to have been "conducted with the assistance of the National Endowment for the Humanities."[11] Despite these credentials, Polos violates the most elementary principles of scholarship. He ignores documented history to create scenes out of pure imagination, presents as facts matters distinctly said not to be so by the journals themselves, and in his footnotes carelessly misquotes Donald Jackson, an outstanding authority on the expedition. For example, without a shred of evidence to support this fanciful account of the party's departure from Camp Wood, Polos writes, "Capt. Clark waves his hat to the small crowd that had gathered to see the sturdy band of adventurers off, but the crowd was too busy watching York, the black giant, doing a fancy clog dance on the stern of the boat!"[12] Continuing in this irresponsible vein, Polos perpetuates the absurd notion that York served Lewis and Clark as a "pathfinder," incorrectly tells the reader that "Clark gave York continued custody of Sacajawea with strict instructions to provide for her needs," and arbitrarily states, in the face of what the journals specifically say to the contrary, that York saved Clark and the Charbonneaus from the flood in the ravine at the Great Falls.[13] As bewildering and as exasperating as this kind of alleged scholarship may be, it is even more bewildering and exasperating to think that both the *Negro History Bulletin* and the National Endowment for the Humanities gave any credence to it.

For almost a century, much nonsense has been written about York, almost all of it derogatory and in need of correction. That of late some writers have been motivated to rescue him from obscurity does not alter the fact that most of what they have written is nonsense, too. As said earlier, the York of the Lewis and Clark journals stands on his own. If new generations of Americans are to be told about him, all they need are the facts, not fairy tales.

III

AN ATTEMPT TO SEE
THE MAN AS HE WAS

10. Childhood in Virginia

When was York born? What was his youth like? Why was he taken on the expedition? At the outset, a disclaimer must be made that there are no fixed and final answers to these and a number of other questions. Because he was a slave and slaves were seldom noticed in public records and family papers, little was written about him while he lived, except in the journals of the expedition. Also, because he was a slave and slaves were forbidden both by custom and by law to be taught to read and write, it is virtually certain he was unable to leave behind a single written word about himself. Yet, while many questions must remain unanswered, the existing sources do contain a surprising amount of information not generally known or previously published. In fact, from them it is possible to reconstruct a rather detailed outline of York's life from the time he was inherited by William Clark until he was reported to have died of cholera in Tennessee, including such major events as his marriage, his falling out with his master, his demotion from the favored status of a body servant to the lowly position of a hired-out slave, his forced separation from his wife, his eventual freedom, and his failure as a free black in a business of his own.

This is far more information to have about a slave who was born two centuries ago than is available about the vast majority of slaves, millions of whom lived and died in anonymity. But while York's life can be seen in outline, an outline is less than satisfactory for those who would like to see him more fully as a person both in terms of the world in which he lived and his probable reactions to it. To attempt to do this, however, means that some speculations must be made, always a risky procedure, although in the case of York there are fortunately two sets of knowns to work with. The first is that he is known to have been a slave boy, later a body servant, later a hired-out slave, and still later a free black who remained in the South. The second is that from many scholarly studies of slavery much is now known about the childhoods of slaves, the relationships of body servants with their masters, the working conditions under which slaves were hired out, and the social and economic barriers faced by free blacks who remained in the South. When these two sets of knowns are brought together, we can understand in greater depth the forces which shaped York's life, just as they shaped the lives of other slaves who had parallel experiences. We can also conjecture within a range of reasonable probabililty that his reactions to those forces would have been much the same as theirs are known to have been.

Although the search for a record of York's birth has proved fruitless, there are substantial reasons to believe he was born a few years after William Clark, whose date of birth was 1 August 1770. For them to have been roughly the same age would have been in keeping with the custom of selecting a young master's body servant from among his former playmates, and for him to have been a few years younger seems to be confirmed by Clark's later reminiscences of him from their childhoods as his "little Negro boy, York."[1] The laws and practices governing the freeing of slaves also point to him having been born after 1770. As will be discussed in more detail later, it was rare for slaves over the age of forty to be freed, and while it is not known when York was finally released from bondage, it is known he was still a slave as late as the spring of 1811. Therefore, even if he had been granted his freedom before the year ended, he should have been no more than forty at the time, making his year of birth 1771 at the very earliest. But this is only an estimate, not a matter of record. Curiously, York himself may not have known the year in which he was born. In explaining why he did not know his own age, Frederick Douglass, a slave who escaped to freedom, recalled: "I never met with a slave who could tell me how old he was. Few slave-mothers know anything of the months of the year, nor of the days of the month. They keep no family records, with marriages, births, and deaths. They measure the ages of their children by spring time, winter time, harvest time, planting time, and the like; but these soon become undistinguishable and forgotten."[2]

All there is to be known of York's parents is contained in Clark's father's will of 24 July 1799. When John Clark died six days later, he left his son

A section of John Clark's will of 24 July 1799. Here he deeds his son William "one Negroe man named York, Also old York, and his Wife Rose, and their two Children Nancy and Juba." *Archives and Records Service, Jefferson County, Kentucky.*

William the family estate of Mulberry Hill near Louisville, all his livestock and plantation equipment, thousands of acres of land in Kentucky and the Illinois country, a still, and eight slaves. Among the slaves were "one Negroe man named York, Also old York, and his Wife Rose, and their two Children Nancy and Juba"[3] Because a copy of the will contains a misleading insertion made later, one writer has concluded that Rose was York's wife, not his mother, but this is incorrect.[4] The original will clearly states that "old York" and Rose were the married couple and the parents of Nancy and Juba. On the other hand, the will does not explicitly say that "old York" and Rose were York's parents as well, although it cannot readily be interpreted in any other way. Surely, York must have received his name from "old York," making it almost certain they were father and son, and while another part of the will raises a question as to whether Rose was York's natural mother, the absence of further information precludes an assumption that his mother was someone else.[5] The will is of further interest on two counts. By differentiating between York, a "Negroe man," and Nancy and Juba, "two Children," it indicates that York was already an adult in 1799, thereby providing an additional reason to think he was born in the 1770s. The names York and Juba are also of interest insofar as they may reveal more about York's parents than appears at first glance.

Except for York and Juba, the names of the twenty slaves mentioned in John Clark's will are for the most part commonplace, such as Harry and Kate, or reflect a whimsical practice of many slaveowners to give classical names to some of their chattels, such as Scippio (*sic*) and Cupid. Juba, however, is a distinct departure from the pattern. Not to be confused with the hand-clapping, knee-slapping slave dance called the juba—from *giouba*, an African dance resembling a jig—the personal name Juba can be traced back to ancient Africa, when at about the time of Christ two successive kings named Juba ruled Numidia, a region roughly corresponding with what is now Algeria.[6] (King Juba I sided with Pompey in one of Rome's civil wars, and King Juba II enjoyed a long reign during which "his subjects marveled that a man could write books and yet rule so well.")[7] What makes this name of special interest is that when slaves were allowed to name their children, they often chose African names as a means of preserving a link with their heritage, and one of the names they chose was Juba.

Could this have been the case with this particular Juba? Could it have been that "old York" and Rose were permitted to name their son and deliberately chose a name of African origin? The possibility cannot be ruled out in view of the unusual combination of circumstances: Juba is an African name, white families seldom gave their slaves African names, and Juba is the only African name among all the slaves mentioned in John Clark's will. Obviously, no conclusion can be drawn regarding this matter, but one cannot resist making a conjecture. If "old York" and Rose did name Juba, then it is reasonable to assume that they probably would have done what other slave parents who were conscious of their heritage are known to have done. They would have instilled in their children an awareness of their African roots, making sure they remembered that not always had black men and women been held in bondage.[8]

Both because of his name and his probable age, "old York" must have been one of the slaves John Clark inherited as a lad of eight when his father died in 1734. Born on a plantation in King and Queen County, Virginia, John Clark lived there until about 1749, when, having married Ann Rogers, he moved west to develop a 410-acre tract of land left him in Albemarle County. At the time he wrote his will in 1799, he was almost seventy-three years old, and two clues point to "old York" having been about the same age. First, unless the word *old* was used only to distinguish the father from the son, it is unlikely John Clark would have applied it to a man much his junior. Second, the name York itself makes it almost certain that he had been born long before on John Clark's father's plantation back in King and Queen County.

A scholar's study of black American names discloses that when the name York was on occasion given to slaves, it was usually adopted from the geography of the general area in which the child was born, although now and then "slave mothers would give their children such names as York and London, according to the point of sail or destination of vessels in the local port at the time of their birth."[9] As it happens, King and Queen County is partly bordered by the York River, is close to York County, and is not far from Yorktown. Unless this is pure coincidence, "old York" was born on John Clark's father's plantation and, in keeping with custom, received his name either from one of these places or from one of the many English ships then plying the York River. This would mean that he went back to John Clark's youth, would have been looked upon fondly as an "old retainer," and may even have been a body servant or house servant who was given the assignment of training his son York along the same lines.

In or about 1757, John and Ann Clark moved east from Albemarle County to a plantation in Caroline County, where William Clark and, almost certainly, York were born. What little is known of their growing up together comes from William Clark Kennerly, Clark's namesake and nephew by marriage, who as a boy in St. Louis listened to his uncle tell stories about his youth.[10] Unfortunately, Kennerly cannot be cited as an unimpeachable source. Clark's stories, as Kennerly recalled them, were not put on paper until many years later, and then not by Kennerly himself but by his daughter. Consequently, the book in which these recollections appear, *Persimmon Hill*, must be approached with caution, for its reliability depends upon the memory of an old man with a romantic turn of mind who at times confused what he had heard directly or from within the family with what he had read about his famous uncles, William and George Rogers Clark. There is, of course, another side of the coin. Kennerly is an extremely rare source in that he actually heard Clark talk about York, and

William Clark Kennerly, Clark's namesake and nephew by marriage. As a boy in St. Louis, he listened to his famous uncle reminisce fondly about York. *From W. C. Kennerly, Persimmon Hill.*

it is not realistic to think that every one of his memories was flawed. On balance, the only choice seems to be to quote from *Persimmon Hill* while, with the help of other sources, trying to distinguish what is probably true from what is probably apocryphal.

Describing his Uncle William as a man with "a hearty, ringing laugh" who enthralled the children gathered around him with stories of his boyhood in Virginia, Kennerly wrote:

William was the youngest of the six Clark brothers. He was a red-haired baby; for one of the early John Clarks had married a red-haired Scotch lady in Maryland, and since that time there has been a red-haired Clark in almost every generation. He was born in 1770 about the time that his older brother George Rogers, a young surveyor, was making his first exploration down the Ohio River; and he grew to be a sturdy lad, tramping the woods in search of small game, fishing in the Rappahannock, and in the long evenings listening to Brother George's tales of his daring campaigns of 1774 in the Dunmore Wars. On school holidays he rode about the countryside, always accompanied by his little Negro boy, York. They often rode into Fredericksburg and stopped at Kenmore House to play with Young Meriwether Lewis, visiting his Uncle Fielding Lewis, brother-in-law to General Washington.[11]

While these are charming stories which are tempting to believe, all the more so because they ostensibly came from the lips of Clark himself, at least one of them must be taken with a grain of salt. Without a doubt, Clark did sit at his older brother's knee and listen to tales of frontier adventure, and he probably did hunt, fish, and ride with young York at his side, but it is most unlikely that he and Lewis knew each other as children. Except for Kennerly, there is no evidence of any kind that they were friends as boys in Virginia; to the contrary, most authorities think they did not meet until as late as 1795 or 1796, when both were grown men serving in the army. Although there is always a possibility Clark recalled experiences from his youth not otherwise recorded, the chances are greater that Kennerly was indulging his tendency to romanticize the past when he described Clark and York riding on school holidays to visit Lewis at his uncle's home in Fredericksburg. Not only was Fredericksburg in a different county from the one in which the Clarks lived, but Lewis moved to Georgia shortly after the Revolution and did not return to Virginia until after the Clarks had emigrated to Kentucky, leaving not very many years for the boys to have developed a lasting friendship. Furthermore, the chances are slim that Clark ever had a school holiday in the usual sense of the words, for his biographer says he was "lacking in formal education," and, like most children who then grew up in rural areas, he seems to have been taught the rudiments of reading, writing, and arithmetic at home.[12]

As for York, he would not have been taught even the rudiments of reading and writing, for in Virginia in colonial times, as well as later, there was vehement opposition to slave literacy on the grounds it could lead to slave insurrections.[13] Nor is it believable, as a direct descendant of William Clark has declared, that York learned to read and write as a grown man. In a paper presented in 1970, William Clark Adreon told his audience York "was taught what he could absorb of the three R's" before being freed, but he offered no documentation either for his claim or for his insinuation that York was slow to learn.[14] Weighing heavily against Adreon is a mass of evidence that throughout the South both punitive laws and public opinion so strongly militated against the teaching of slaves only a very small percentage of them ever became literate.[15] Indeed, so rare was a literate slave that an 1820 St. Louis newspaper advertisement for one who had run away called attention to the man's ability to read "a little" as a certain way to identify him.[16] However, while York would never have received any classroom instruction, he most assuredly had to attend the hardest school of all—the school of slavery, with lessons far more difficult to learn than those ever assigned any white child.

Frederick Douglass, a slave who fled to the North and became a powerful spokesman for abolition, remembered his childhood until about the age of eight as happy, and other sources confirm these early years to have been for the most part sheltered insofar as little or no work was required of the small ones.[17] Even until the age of twelve or so the boys and girls performed no heavy labor, although they often were given regular chores to do, such as weeding family gardens, carrying water to the field hands, and helping the older women clean and cook.[18] (This was in marked contrast to what observers from abroad had to say about "the cruel fate which befalls poor children of their age in the mining and manufacturing districts of England.")[19] Yet, while on the surface life seemed placid and even carefree, in the slave cabins a process painful for parents and children alike inevitably took place.

Depending upon the individual circumstances, slave children were sooner or later confronted with the shattering realization that they were different in two fundamental ways: they were black and they were property. Sometimes the revelation came when they noticed a white child who had previously shown no consciousness of color suddenly withdraw behind an attitude of superiority; sometimes it came when they saw a parent helpless to reply to a reprimand or even bodily punishment from a white master or overseer; sometimes it came when they heard of a person of their race sold and sent away like one of the animals of the fields; and sometimes it came quietly when a mother or father had to tell them they were doomed to be slaves for the rest of their lives, inferior to all those who had had the good fortune to have been born white. As traumatic as these moments must have been, they were only the beginning of slave children's educations. From then on, it was imperative they learn that unless they conformed to the system they could not survive.

When and how the boy York faced the bitter moment of awareness that he was a slave is unknown, but face it he surely did. And whether or not he voiced the question in the same words Frederick Douglass used, he surely asked it in some form: "*Why am I a slave? Why are some people slaves, and others masters?*"[20] The answer York was given was never recorded, as it was with Douglass, who was told God made white people to be masters and black people slaves, an explanation totally incomprehensible to a child who had been taught that God was good. But no matter how York's question was answered, it was only the first of many heartbreaking lessons all slave parents knew their child had to learn as a matter, literally, of life and death. Because they knew there was no place within the system for the slave who refused to submit to it, they had to blunt their child's natural aggressions lest he or she later in life strike a white person in anger, bringing disaster crashing down. They had to drill their child to accept humiliations passively, to carry out the most capricious orders without hesitation, and always when in the presence of whites to wear "a deferential mask."[21] By one means or another—submissive example, stern lectures, and not infrequently physical force—parents had to restructure their child's basic personality, with the price paid for suppressing normal human emotions an apparently high incidence of psychological disorders among the slave population.[22]

To be sure, some slaves learned to cope better than others, and all signs point to York having been one of them. Not only did he survive his schooling in slavery, but he actually succeeded to the extent of being selected for one of the most privileged of all slave positions, a body servant. This was no mean accomplishment and in itself tends to refute William Clark Adreon's insinuation that he was slow to learn. As is known to have been true of many other slaves, York probably was quick to see the hopelessness of his situation and adapted to it as best he could. As is also known to have been true of many other slaves, he seems to have understood that while the system itself was cold and impersonal, one could still form strong attachments to members of the other race. Not the least remarkable of all the peculiar aspects of slavery is that many close and lifelong friendships developed between masters and slaves, particularly between masters and their body servants, with some becoming so devoted to each other they were buried side by side.[23]

York's childhood on the Clark family's plantation in Caroline County was probably much the same as the childhoods experienced by most slave boys who grew up in the rural South. As they did, he would have worn a homespun shirt reaching to his knees, gone barefooted the greater part of the year, lived in a log cabin with a dirt floor, done a few chores, romped and wrestled with the other slave children, roamed the fields, learned to swim in a river or pond, and generally run free in the manner familiar to country-bred youngsters everywhere. During his early years, he would have spent many of his days with William Clark, for not only was it common for black and white children of the same plantation to play together, but it was also customary for a body servant to be selected from among the young master's playmates. (These were the years Clark later told William Clark Kennerly he spent tramping the woods in search of game, fishing in the Rappahannock, and riding about the countryside "always accompanied by his little Negro boy, York.") Based upon what is known of other friendships between white and black children, the two boys would have been largely oblivious of their differences of color and caste, and certainly of what those differences would soon lead to in making one the master and the other a body servant.[24] And if, like other children, they played at being soldiers and frontiersmen, they would have been equally oblivious of the fact that one day their wildest dreams of adventure would be more than fulfilled.

Reports of the momentous events taking place in the far-off world beyond the plantation's boundaries could not have failed to fire the boys' imaginations, for they were children of the American Revolution and all five of Clark's older brothers were away fighting the British. (The second oldest, George Rogers Clark, was leading his Virginia troops to such stunning victories against the British and Indians in the Old Northwest that he would win fame as one of the most brilliant generals of the war.) From 1775 to 1781—or from the time Clark was five until he was eleven—deeds of heroism in battles lost and won would have been the talk of the plantation, even in the slave quarters, where it would have been no secret that black soldiers and sailors were fighting with the Continental

Howard Pyle's *George
Rogers Clark on His Way to
Kaskaskia*. William's
older brother, shown
here with his Virginia
troops in the back-
ground, was the hero of
the American Revolu-
tion in the Old North-
west. *The Thomas
Gilcrease Institute of
American History and
Art, Tulsa, Oklahoma.*

forces. With the coming of peace after Cornwallis surrendered at York-town, there still would have been many exciting events to discuss. All of Clark's brothers returned home with stories of their adventures, and one of them returned with glowing reports of the country around the Falls of the Ohio, where a small settlement he had founded during the war was growing into the town of Louisville. Convinced that great opportunities lay waiting in the fertile Ohio Valley, and having acquired there, in his words, an "unprecedented Quantity of the finest Lands in the western world," George Rogers Clark persuaded his father to leave Virginia and go west with his family and slaves to a new life in Kentucky.[25]

11. Growing to Manhood in Kentucky

Custom would have dictated that the Clarks chose York to be William's body servant at about the time the family moved to Kentucky. The move started late in 1784, when William was fourteen and York evidently several years younger, which would have made him approximately the age when slave boys and girls were forced to put childhood behind and enter an entirely new phase of their lives. The age of twelve was a watershed year for slave children, the time when most were sent to the fields to work while a fortunate few were singled out for domestic duty in the "big house."[1] Only slaves could fully appreciate the significance of the moment when the decision was made as to the direction in which the child would go. The fields meant a life of hard physical labor unrelieved by comforts and privileges, whereas assignment to the "big house" meant not only material advantages, such as better food and clothing, but also a degree of personal consideration as a result of living and working close to the masters and mistresses. So entirely different were the worlds of the field hands and the house slaves that when a slave boy in Kentucky was chosen to be a young master's playmate, with everyone knowing it would lead to him becoming a domestic servant, he was looked upon as "the star of the plantation."[2] Like that boy, York must have been the star of the Clark plantation when word came down to the slave quarters that he was to be young Master William's body servant.

From the moment York stepped into his new role, his life would have changed dramatically. He would have enjoyed special status in the hierarchy of the Clark family's slaves, because just as "house servants formed a class quite distinct from, and socially above, the field hands," body servants were the elite among the household staffs.[3] He would have eaten much the same food as the Clarks themselves, and he would have cast away his homespun shirt for clothes similar to those worn by his young master, although probably in the form of hand-me-downs from Clark's older brothers. His training would have prepared him to be a combination of a valet and a confidant, one who would later serve his master at the table, shave him, assist him in dressing, and attend to all his needs.[4] His training would also have prepared him to accompany his master on business and social rounds, during which he often would be present when matters requiring discretion were discussed. He would have been instilled with a sense of responsibility for Clark's safety, would have been told to stay near him day and night, and may have been selected in the first place partly because he showed signs of becoming unusually large and strong.[5] Moreover, if he were a typical body servant—and there is no reason to think he was not—he would have developed highly polished manners and in all likelihood would have spoken in a way which would have surprised those writers who have given him a comic "darkie" dialect, for it is a matter of record that many slaves who were raised with white children and served as domestics pronounced English little differently than did Southern whites.[6]

In October 1784, John Clark and his "numerous family of children and servants" left Caroline County and traveled overland and by boat to Pittsburgh, where ice in the Ohio River delayed their journey until early in 1785.[7] When the trip resumed and the Clarks were descending the river, not long before arriving at the Falls of the Ohio they almost became a part of the Indian troubles they would soon hear so much about. Seeing a large canoe filled with Indians, they were not alarmed, for the tribes then hunting in Kentucky were said to be at peace. John Clark therefore had no reason to be concerned when later the same day he left his family and went ashore with one of his slaves to visit the dwelling of a man he knew from back in Virginia. Finding that he was away from home and that his wife was disinclined to offer hospitality for the night, the Clarks continued on their way only to learn within a day or so that on the evening of their visit the Indians attacked the farm, burned the cabins to the ground, and massacred all but two of the inhabitants.

The raid the Clarks and their slaves narrowly missed was not an isolated incident. Although few Indians lived in Kentucky, they prized it as a rich hunting ground, with tribes to the north, west, and south resenting the

Like these settlers descending the Ohio River, the Clark family traveled by boat from Pittsburgh to Kentucky in 1785. *The Filson Club, Louisville, Kentucky.*

flood of white settlers. As a result, in the words of one who moved there just three years after the Clarks, the topics of daily conversation were of "midnight butcheries, captivities, and horse stealings," and a subsequent report to the secretary of war informed him that between 1783 and 1790 some 1,500 Kentuckians had been killed by Indians.[8] By the time the Clarks reached the Falls of the Ohio, the entire household, including the boys William and York, knew from firsthand experience that they had arrived on the tumultuous frontier and had left the gentle ways of Virginia far behind.

Few details have been handed down about the settling of Mulberry Hill, the name of John and Ann Clark's new home several miles south of Louisville, but it is known that the main house was a six-room log structure standing on a 290-acre tract of land.[9] In its early stages, Mulberry Hill

Mulberry Hill, the Clark family's home a few miles south of Louisville. From an old photograph taken when the building had fallen into disrepair. *The Filson Club, Louisville, Kentucky.*

seems to have been more a farm than a plantation (at least William Clark later remembered it as such), and, like other Kentucky farms, the usual crops of corn, oats, rye, tobacco, hemp, and flax would have been grown, with turnips, peas, pumpkins, and sweet potatoes prominent among the vegetables raised for the table.[10] A frontier farm being located at a distance from the nearest neighbors, the Clark family—and then the word *family* meant the slaves as well—would have been a closely knit and self-sufficient group. The women, white and black, would have carded and spun wool, made their own soap, laundered clothes by boiling them in huge kettles, and preserved food as best they could by smoking meat, storing vegetables in a root cellar, and keeping dairy products fresh in a springhouse. They would, however, have been spared one usual task: because windows in pioneer Kentucky were made of oiled paper instead of glass, they would not have had to clean them.

The men, white and black, would have cleared fields, put up fences, tended the livestock, cut wood for the fireplaces, hunted deer and wild turkeys, and constructed farm buildings, including one for the still William would later inherit. Reflecting upon the simplicity of rural life in those days, the author of a book on slavery in Kentucky has written that masters and slaves "worked together in the fields, marched together against the Indians, and slept side by side in family cemeteries."[11] While it is doubtful York was one of those slaves who marched against the Indians, it is conceivable he helped to repel an Indian raid at home. According to a descendant of Frances Clark, William's youngest sister, Mulberry Hill "was at one time attacked by the Indians and the logs are full of bullet holes as the result."[12] (As simple and free of formality as life on the Kentucky frontier may have appeared to be, York could not have failed to realize that beneath the surface the harsh undercurrent of slavery continued to flow. Just a year after his arrival at Mulberry Hill, word would have traveled quickly through the black grapevine of a slave named Tom in nearby Louisville who was condemned to death for having stolen nothing more than "two and three-fourths yards of cambric and some ribbon and thread.")[13]

The Clarks would come to enjoy a reputation for gracious and generous hospitality, but at first most of their energy and the energy of their slaves had to go into developing Mulberry Hill. With so much to be done, the usual lines of demarcation between the duties of slaves were probably broken down, and York could have spent more time as a laborer or field hand than as a body servant. There would, however, have been some free time, and Clark and York can be assumed to have used theirs as other Kentucky youths of that era are known to have done, in hunting, fishing, and becoming familiar with the ways of the rivers and woods. While they could not have realized it then, much of what they were learning by living on the frontier would stand them in good stead during the expedition to the Pacific. In the case of Clark, the journals reveal that he was a crack shot, a fine horseman, an expert handler of boats, had an unerring sense of direction, and could take care of himself when alone in the wilds. In the case of York, less is known of his wilderness skills, although in view of the criteria Lewis and Clark laid down requiring their men to be expert woodsmen, there can be little question he had mastered many of them.

Between 1789 and 1796, Mulberry Hill saw less and less of William Clark, who as a young man of nineteen left home to follow in the military footsteps of his older brothers. First serving briefly as a volunteer with a group of Kentucky militiamen who went out to subdue Indians north of the Ohio River, he subsequently participated in Indian actions under General Charles Scott, being described at the time in a letter to his brother Jonathan as "a youth of solid and promising parts, and as brave as Caesar."[14] The manner in which he rose through the ranks is uncertain, but on 6 March 1792, before he had turned twenty-two, President Washington nominated him to be a lieutenant in the United States Army. During his career as a regular army officer, he fought with distinction under General Anthony Wayne at the Battle of Fallen Timbers and delivered a letter protesting Spanish activities on the American side of the Mississippi to the Spanish Governor General at New Madrid in what is now Missouri. Before he resigned from the army as either a first lieutenant or brevet captain on 1 July 1796, he commanded a rifle company to which a young officer named Meriwether Lewis was posted. While they apparently then met for the first time and knew each other for only a few months, a lasting friendship was formed, one eventually leading Lewis to ask Clark to share command of the expedition.

Where was York during these years? It is impossible to say, for he does not turn up even once in any of the diaries Clark kept off and on when he was serving in the army. Because these diaries, like the journals he kept while on the expedition, focus more on places and events than on people, York could have been with him and merely not mentioned. But what would appear to be more plausible is that he stayed behind at Mulberry Hill, where much work remained to be done and his strength would have been useful. However, this is only a conjecture. Quite simply, York's whereabouts during this period of his master's life are not known, and it is only after Clark's resignation from the army and return to Mulberry Hill that any reference can be found to them once more being together.

Two reasons motivated Clark to resign his commission in 1796: the state of his health and the state of George Rogers Clark's financial affairs. In 1811, he wrote Nicholas Biddle that after he had gone back to Mulberry Hill he "lived several years in bad health."[15] At the same time, his brother's mounting financial problems played a part in his decision to return to civilian life. During the Revolution, as the general commanding Virginia troops fighting in the Old Northwest, George Rogers had pledged his personal credit in order to provide food and supplies for his men, but after the war the Virginia legislature had refused to honor the debts, claiming they were obligations of the new federal government. When neither Virginia nor Congress appropriated any funds, George Rogers was soon entangled in a web of lawsuits which threatened to impoverish him, and by 1796 he had become deeply embittered and depressed. Not long after leaving the army, William began to travel extensively on his brother's behalf, trying to satisfy creditors and settle legal actions. In 1797, he wrote, "I have rode for Bro. Geo in the course of this past year upwards of 3,000 miles continually on the pad, attempting to save him."[16]

Years later, William Clark told his nephew William Clark Kennerly that during this busy period of his life he "had ridden back and forth through the Cumberland Gap to tidewater Virginia in his brother's interest, York riding at his side."[17] Although Kennerly's memory cannot always be trusted, in this instance the custom of having body servants travel with their masters gives credibility to his words. Because it was all but unheard of for a gentleman to go far from home without his body servant along to ease the traveling discomforts of those days, and also because Clark was not feeling well at the time, it would have been highly irregular for York not to have attended him on the many trips he took between 1796 and 1803.

In 1796 and 1797, Clark—and with little question York as well—rode endlessly over frontier roads in those parts of the Middle West later to become the states of Indiana and Illinois. In 1798, he went down the Ohio and Mississippi Rivers to New Orleans, where he purchased and sent back to Mulberry Hill a barrel of sugar and a barrel of coffee, at the same time obtaining a passport from Spanish authorities permitting him to travel by ship to New York. During the years 1800, 1801, and 1802, he went back and forth between Kentucky and the East, having, in his words, "frequent Reasons to Visit the Eastern States & Washington where I became Acquainted with the Presidt. Mr. Jefferson."[18] Clark was introduced to the president by his friend Meriwether Lewis, then Jefferson's private secretary, and while it can only be surmised that York met Jefferson and Lewis at this time, it is reasonable to think he did. It is also reasonable to think he was on hand when Clark met the two young cousins, Julia Hancock and Harriet Kennerly, who would be his first and second wives. William Clark Kennerly says Clark described this meeting as having taken place when he and York were traveling back and forth through the Cumberland Gap to tidewater Virginia, and Kennerly's account is corroborated by his older sister, Mary Kennerly Taylor. In a letter to Eva Emery Dye, Mrs. Taylor wrote:

> Uncle Clark has often told me of his first meeting with Julia and Harriett [*sic*]. they were nearly the same age, Julia a few months older than Harriett. The girls were both riding on one horse & trying their best to get the horse to go, both using switches to urge him on, but he would not move. Clark riding by, the girls called on him to help them. he helped the children, leading the horse for some time & when he mounted his own theirs followed. this was his first introduction to the girls. I have often heard him speak of it & say though a very young man he made up his mind that Julia should be his wife.[19]

William would marry Julia, who was also called Judith, in 1808, and after her death in 1820 he would marry Harriet, then a widow, the following year. But these events were hidden in the future, while at the moment he and his brother Jonathan were tirelessly engaged in efforts to save George Rogers from bankruptcy. In order to prevent all of the beleaguered general's possessions from being seized by creditors, most of the huge land claims he held in Kentucky and the western country were transferred to William, who for the same reason became the principal heir of their father's estate upon his death in 1799. (It also appears that some of George Roger's slaves, who as property were subject to seizure, were conveyed to William as part of these transactions.)[20] Despite William's sizeable inheritance, legal costs and other expenses continued to deplete his resources to the point where in 1803, in need of additional funds, he sold Mulberry Hill to Jonathan. By then, however, he was no longer living there. At some time before 12 December 1802, he had moved in with George Rogers, who had built a small house in Clarksville, a nearly deserted village across the river from Louisville at the foot of the Falls of the Ohio.[21]

At Clark's Point, as the location of the house was called, William must have felt at home surrounded by the many familiar objects reflecting his brother's lifelong fascination with natural history, including part of the petrified backbone of a mammoth which stood outside the front door and was sometimes used by George Rogers as a seat.[22] York, too, must have felt

Julia Hancock Clark, William Clark's first wife. During the expedition, he named the Judith River in Montana for her. They were married in 1808. *From W. C. Kennerly, Persimmon Hill.*

Harriet Kennerly Radford Clark, William Clark's second wife. Clark's two wives were cousins he met while visiting Virginia before the expedition. After Julia died in 1820, he married Harriet, then a widow, the following year. *From W. C. Kennerly, Persimmon Hill.*

at home with "Cupid and Venus, George Rogers' faithful couple," slaves he had known from Mulberry Hill, if not from his childhood back in Virginia.[23] Here in Clarksville, in July 1803, William Clark received an invitation to adventure quite similar to one his older brother had been sent some twenty years earlier. Then, in 1783, Thomas Jefferson had written to ask George Rogers whether he might be interested in leading a small party to explore the West, but he had declined because of the financial problems already closing in on him. Now, on 18 July 1803, William accepted without hesitation Meriwether Lewis's invitation to join him on the expedition President Jefferson was sending to the Pacific. Replying to Lewis's letter the day after it arrived, he wrote, "This is an undertaking fraited with many dificulties, but My friend I do assure you that no man lives whith whome I would perfur to undertake Such a Trip &c. as your self, and I

Sketch of George Rogers Clark's home in Clarksville, Indiana Territory, where William Clark was living by late 1802. It was here he received the letter from Lewis asking him to share command of the expedition. *From W. H. English, Conquest of the Northwest, 1778–1783, and Life of Gen. George Rogers Clark.*

shall arrange my matters as well as I can against your arrival here."[24] One of the matters he had to arrange was what to do about York.

What prompted Clark—and, indeed, Lewis as well—to take York on the expedition? Although neither ever referred to the decision in writing, it had to have been made when Lewis arrived at the Falls of the Ohio and the selection of personnel was discussed. In his letter to Clark, Lewis had specified that they should look for "good hunters, stout, healthy, unmarried men, accustomed to the woods, and capable of bearing bodily fatigue in a pretty considerable degree," and later, as Private Alexander Willard recalled, the captains winnowed out more than one hundred men who could not meet their physical standards.[25] It therefore seems safe to assume that York measured up to most or all of the requirements, for it would have been totally out of character for either Lewis or Clark to have jeopardized the outcome of what they knew would be a high-risk mission by taking along a man whose lack of wilderness skills or stamina might prove to be a weak link in the chain. To be sure, on the way up the Missouri Clark described York as fat and unable to hike as fast as he did, and this remains an enigma, but on balance one must conclude that the captains viewed his unusual strength and other qualities as more important than what seems to have been, at least early in the journey, his less than trim condition.[26]

While Clark's description of York as fat contradicts the traditional image of him as a man of superb physique—an image epitomized by Charles M. Russell's painting of him being scrutinized by curious Indians—the original sources leave no doubt he was of "very large size," had extraordinary "powers Strength &c.," and moved with such agility when he danced that the Indians were astonished "So large a man should be active."[27] These physical attributes would have been viewed as assets for any exploration, especially one which would have to propel itself up rivers mainly by sheer muscle power. But an even more significant consideration must have entered into Lewis and Clark's evaluation of him. Knowing with certainty they would encounter many emergencies, including the likelihood of conflict with Indians, they would never have allowed York to accompany them unless they had been confident that he would be steady and reliable in moments of crisis. In itself, this says much about the man.

Jefferson's long and detailed letter of instructions to Lewis may have been still another reason Lewis and Clark decided to take York along. When they reviewed all the president expected of them above and beyond the overriding responsibility of leading the expedition to the Pacific —keeping journals, taking observations of latitude and longitude, recording details of the flora, fauna, and climate of the country they would cross, and dealing as ambassadors with the Indian tribes they would meet along the way—they may have foreseen that York, an experienced body servant, could free them of many hours they would otherwise have to devote to the petty details of daily living.[28] But this is only a speculation. The facts, as they are known, reveal no more than that York was chosen where many other men were not, and that in the course of the difficult journey he proved Lewis and Clark's judgment to have been right.

12. The Post-Expedition Years and York's Fall from Grace

From the time Lewis arrived at the Falls of the Ohio in October 1803 until the expedition returned from the Pacific in September 1806, York was the only black member of a small, tightly-knit company of men who were single-mindedly committed to crossing the continent. During those years, he not only saw and did things seldom seen and done by any man, but he also enjoyed a taste of freedom and respect seldom enjoyed by any slave. Working, eating, sleeping, and chancing his life shoulder to shoulder with white companions, he apparently was spared the usual indignities of discrimination, to which it can be added that as the exploration progressed he seems to have become more and more accepted by the group. As unrealistic as it would be to think that all of his companions treated him the same—Sergeant Gass, for one, is known to have disliked blacks—it nevertheless is true that nowhere in any of the journals, including Sergeant Gass's, is a derogatory remark made about him or is an act suggesting racial prejudice reported.[1] If nothing else, this seems to say that while beyond the frontier the white members of the expedition, many of whom were from slave states, were able to ignore the usual boundaries of bias. But those boundaries quickly closed in again the moment the explorers appeared from out of the wilderness and York set foot in St. Louis.

Having experienced a degree of freedom he had never known before, having had a close relationship with white companions, and having been admired by the Indians as "big medicine," York was suddenly plunged back into what a man who had also been born into bondage called "the dark night of slavery."[2] When he arrived in St. Louis on 23 September 1806, York reentered a world where he was deemed to be inferior in every way and where, as a reminder of how fragile the underpinnings of a slave's life were, a student of slavery in that town has remarked, "While his master may have been a kindly man, the Negro still was constantly and endlessly

A partial view of St. Louis, as engraved on an 1817 bank note. *Missouri Historical Society.*

aware that he was property, subject to the whims of man and market."[3] During the month Lewis and Clark remained in St. Louis, York seems to have shared the warm welcome given all the returned explorers, but he still would have been required to observe the slave regulations laid down by the Code of 1804, which differed only slightly from the codes of other communities throughout the South at the time. Under that code, he would have been forbidden to leave Clark's temporary place of residence without a pass, forbidden to carry the firearm he had used on the expedition, forbidden to administer medicine to any white person (many Southerners had a fear of being poisoned by their slaves), and, of course, forbidden to raise his hand, no matter how provoked, against any member of the white race.[4] Hemmed in on every side by these and other regulations, York could not have helped but contrast the life he had known beyond the frontier with his life back in civilization. As was the case with every other slave, he also could not have helped but wonder what it would be like to be free.

A standard part of Lewis and Clark folklore handed down as gospel from generation to generation is that Clark rewarded York with freedom upon the expedition's return. As best can be determined, the first who stated this to be a fact was Elliott Coues in 1893.[5] However, despite constant repetition ever since, it is not true. To the contrary, York remained in bondage for at least five more years, during which time he fell from the

Old illustration of a slave auction. The auction block was a constant reminder to all slaves that they were "subject to the whims of man and market." *State Historical Society of Missouri, Columbia.*

highly favored status of a body servant to one of the lowest of all slave positions, a hired-out slave. Why Clark did not free him in 1806 is hard to understand when the words he had used in 1802 to free a slave named Ben are examined. Then, in the instrument of manumission, Clark had explained that he was setting Ben free both "in consideration of the services already rendered to me" and because philosophically he regarded "perpetual involuntary servitude to be contrary of principles of natural Justice," two reasons which certainly should have applied to York as well.[6] Nevertheless, as inequitable and inconsistent as this seems to have been, it gives us no license to judge Clark piously with hindsight. A product of his time and place, he probably was as ambivalent about slavery and the freeing of slaves as were many troubled slaveholders. Torn between private doubts and public practices, it was a rare man who did not vacillate and a rarer man who went so far as to free even some his slaves.[7]

On October 21, the expedition having been disbanded, Lewis and Clark set out from St. Louis for Washington, where the applause and honors due returning heroes awaited them. Their traveling party included, among others, York, Sergeant Ordway, Francis Labiche, the Mandan chief Sheheke who had come down the Missouri with them, and a delegation of Osage chiefs on their way to meet President Jefferson. The group first visited Governor William Henry Harrison in Vincennes, where York was in the presence of the future president, then stopped briefly to pay respects to George Rogers Clark at his home in Clarksville. Continuing on to Louisville, they stayed with Clark's relatives for several days before departing without Clark and York, who would resume the journey after spending Christmas with their families. Recalling what he was told of York's reception on the day he and his master appeared at Locust Grove, the home of

Crayon drawing by C. B. J. Fevret de Saint Mémin of Sheheke, the Mandan chief who accompanied Lewis and Clark down the Missouri and visited President Jefferson in Washington. *American Philosophical Society.*

Clark's older sister Lucy and her husband William Croghan, William Clark Kennerly wrote:

> York was in the quarters unpacking his Indian trophies to the "oh's" and "ah's" and prideful joy of his parents, Old York and Nancy, the cook. Cupid and Venus, George Rogers' faithful couple, leaving Old Henry at home to take care of their master, came over to Locust Grove to rejoice with them. Little work was done that first day, and candles burned late in the cabins as York recited his adventures with dramatic pose. He took much pleasure, too, in the fact of the buckskins' being abolished and in seeing his master again in ruffled shirt, silken hose, and buckled pumps.[8]

Kennerly's memory of this occasion is faulty in at least one detail: John Clark's will identifies York's mother as Rose, whereas here she is Nancy. A Nancy was, however, named in the will as the daughter of "old York" and Rose, and if the same person her role as the cook for the Croghans would mean that she, like her brother York, had risen to one of the more privileged of slave positions. Despite Kennerly's apparent confusion between Rose and Nancy, his description of York's delight at seeing his master properly dressed again has the ring of reality. As a body servant, he not only would have taken pride in Clark's appearance, but he also would have taken pains to make sure Clark's wardrobe was in perfect condition for his visit to the nation's capital. While no document specifically says York was with Clark when he left Louisville, there is every reason to believe that in his capacity as a body servant he went along, just as there is every reason to believe that Clark himself would have made sure "my man York," as he so frequently referred to him in the journals, was appropriately attired.

Reaching Washington on 21 January 1807, three weeks later than Lewis, Clark was still in time to be lionized and to receive along with his friend more tangible expressions of the country's gratitude for their historic achievement. Although young men only in their thirties, both were appointed to high posts. Lewis was named Governor of the Territory of Upper Louisiana, while Clark became the territory's brigadier general of militia, as well as Superintendent of Indian Affairs for all but a few of the huge territory's many Indian tribes. Early in March, Clark left Washington and traveled to Fotheringay, the Hancock family's plantation near Fincastle, Virginia, where he became engaged to Julia Hancock, one of the two young cousins he had met years before when they were riding a balky horse. Then he proceeded to St. Louis, where he and Governor Lewis were to reside and discharge their new duties.

The next few years, while Clark and York were living in St. Louis, seem to have been when the word-of-mouth account handed down from "the time of Governors Lewis and Clark" has York the favorite of the taverns, capping the tales of trappers "with tales more marvelous still." What little else there is to be known of him during this period comes from a sparse scattering of documents written in 1808 and 1809, one of which falls just short of saying he was with Clark when Clark returned to Virginia to marry Julia in 1808. At least it definitely places him with the newlyweds when they and a party of relatives, friends, and slaves left Louisville by boat for St. Louis on 2 June 1808. In a letter written from Louisville on that date, George R. C. Sullivan told John O'Fallon, Clark's nephew, "York goes down the river with his master and Molly [a slave] and all the rest."[9] Evidently confirming that York was with his master when he was married, William Clark Kennerly's recollections of what he had been told have York acting as the major-domo of the couple's servants on their honeymoon. Describing the arrival of the Clarks in St. Louis, when Julia's maids were scurrying about with her many pieces of luggage, Kennerly wrote, "And, of course, overseeing all was York, who considered himself personally responsible for the Clark household."[10]

After Sullivan's letter, York's name turns up only twice in documents written in 1808 and 1809. In August 1808, Lewis entered in his account book: "Gave York this sum to bear his expences when he went in surch of a negroe man of Genl. Clark's in St. Charles dist. $4."[11] In August 1809, York's name appears again in a settlement of account between Lewis and Clark, but this entry by Lewis has every appearance of referring back to the money he had advanced York the year before. (He wrote: "To this sum lent York to surch for a negroe man. $1.")[12] It therefore cannot be established that York was still with Clark in St. Louis in 1809, a point raised only because still another document written in 1809 seems to be significant in failing to mention York when reporting events where in his capacity as a body servant he should have been present. Up to this time, there has been no hint of any kind that the relationship between Clark and York was other than normal, with York continuing in daily attendance upon his master. But now a clue comes along to raise doubts that by the fall of 1809 all was still the same between the two men.

On 21 September 1809, Clark, Julia, and their infant son, Meriwether Lewis Clark, left St. Louis for Virginia, where Julia and the child would visit her family while Clark continued on to Washington and Philadelphia to conduct business. In a memorandum book Clark kept throughout the trip, he noted that two slaves accompanied them, which is only to be expected as the journey was long and servants were invariably taken with their masters and mistresses both to assist with carriage travel over crude roads and to make life easier at the many overnight stops along the way. What is unexpected is that neither of these slaves was York. Instead, their names were Chloe and Scot.[13] Because it was highly unusual for a master to travel without his body servant and also because Clark gave no explanation for York's absence, we are left to wonder why he was not along. The answer may lie in a virtually unknown letter written in 1811, which has never been published and contains many surprises. It can be interpreted to mean that by perhaps as early as 1809, and almost surely no later than the spring of 1810, York was no longer a member of the Clark household in St. Louis. It tells us he had been sent to Louisville to be near his wife, of whom no other source makes any mention. It also tells us he had been hired to a man who had misused him. Most startling of all, it discloses that York and his master had had a falling out so serious that York feared he could never regain Clark's good graces.

In a letter from Louisville dated 13 May 1811, John O'Fallon, Clark's nineteen-year-old nephew, wrote his uncle:

> Since I have been down which is about five weeks I have made frequent enquiries relative to the conduct of York since his living here and in justice to him must assert that all the information I have been able to gather contribute strongly to prove that his conduct is (has been) such as entitles him to credit—The term for which he was hired to Mr. Young yesterday expired but I believe agreable to request Mr. Fitzhugh has again hired him to a Mr. Mitchell living about seven miles from this place—I believe your views for permitting him to live here in preference to St. Louis were that he might be with his wife—but I imagine now as there is a great probability that the owner of said wife will within a few

Eng.d by A.H.Ritchie

Steel engraving of John
O'Fallon and his signature.
William Clark's nephew,
O'Fallon was much younger
than seen here when in 1811
he wrote to inform his uncle
of York's mistreatment as a
hired-out slave in Louisville.
*From J. T. Scharf, History of St.
Louis City and County.*

months leave this quarter for Natches [Natchez] carrying with him the
said wife your views on the score of York not [now?] being answered it
will be needless to hire him out for a term equal to that for which he was
last.

I apprehend that he has been indifferently clothed if at all by Young as
appearance satisfactorily prove—he appears wretched under the fear
that he has incurred your displeasure and which he despairs he will ever
remove—I am confident he sorely repent of whatever misconduct of his
that might have led to such a breach and moreover has considerably
amended and in fine deem it not unreasonable to recommend his situation to your consideration.[14]

O'Fallon's letter fairly bursts with entirely new and unexpected information. It tells us things about York not even hinted at by any other source:

he was a slave as late as 1811, he had a wife, he had been stripped of his duties as a body servant, and in his relationship with Clark there had been at least one very stormy moment. At the same time, the letter raises a number of questions for which there are only partial answers. Why was he in disgrace? When had he been sent to Louisville? When had he married? Why had he been hired to a man who treated him shabbily? And, underlying all, just how deep was the relationship between him and his master?

York's and Clark's lives had long been intertwined, apparently starting as childhood playmates and continuing through years of daily intimacy as master and body servant. In addition, on the expedition they had shared the kind of adventures and experiences which normally bind men together. Although the businesslike journal Clark kept on the journey to the Pacific gives little insight into their personal feelings, two entries in particular tend to support the belief their relationship was close. On the day of departure from Camp Wood, Clark used the expression "2 Self," giving the impression he had come to think of York and himself as inseparable. Also, when York feared that Clark was in danger during the fierce storm at the Great Falls, he was, in Clark's words, so "greatly agitated, for our wellfar" he continued to hunt for him while the storm raged. To this it can be added that years later William Clark Kennerly often heard his uncle speak fondly and with genuine affection of York as a faithful retainer who had long been a vivid figure in his life. When all of these things are considered—and bearing in mind that many masters and their body servants developed close relationships—it is only natural to think a strong bond had been forged between the two men, one which would not easily have been broken.[15]

What then could York have done to have so displeased Clark that he allowed his longtime companion and body servant to be reduced to the lowly state of a neglected hired slave? The answer is unknown, but in Clark's eyes the matter must have been extremely serious. Curiously, although O'Fallon was a member of the Clark family, he seems to have been totally in the dark as to the cause of the rift, referring only vaguely to "whatever misconduct of his that might have led to such a breach." On several other matters, however, he is quite clear. He leaves no doubt York was tormented by the thought he was to blame for what had happened and that he despaired of ever being forgiven. He also leaves no doubt that by his subsequent behavior York had tried to redeem himself with his master. And he goes so far as to enter a plea on York's behalf, evidently having been touched by seeing for himself York's miserable condition. Nevertheless, O'Fallon gives no insight of any kind into what had come between the two men, nor does any other source in all the literature having to do with Lewis and Clark even allude to the incident. To the contrary, all other sources convey the moonlight-and-magnolias impression that the relationship between Clark and York was always one of perfect harmony, with not the slightest shadow of a disagreement ever coming between them.

York had indeed fallen on hard times. In addition to having been dismissed from his position as a body servant, he had been ill-used by the man for whom he had to work, having been "indifferently clothed if at all." At the same time, he was facing an ordeal all slaves dreaded but were helpless to prevent: the forced separation of husbands and wives. O'Fallon's letter is one of the most informative of all documents having to do with York, telling us much more about his later life than has ever been known or suspected. Yet, because it provides no background on either the hiring of slaves or the fragile nature of slave marriages, these subjects are worth examining briefly in terms of their relevance to York. Not only can they provide a basis for estimating when he may have been sent to Louisville, but they can also give us a better understanding of just how far down the ladder of fortune he had dropped. Furthermore, a look at the practice of hiring slaves out—once frowned on by many Southerners because it often led to exploitation and abuse—raises the question of what Clark could have had in mind when he requested Mr. Fitzhugh, who apparently was his brother-in-law, to send York out to work.[16]

When slaves were hired out, they almost invariably were assigned to employers for a year under written contracts specifying the amount of money to be paid the owners, as well as, ironically in the case of York, requiring the employers "to keep them well clothed."[17] According to O'Fallon, York's term of hire to a man named Young had expired the day before he wrote Clark, or on 12 May 1811. Therefore, had York been hired to Young for the customary one-year period, he had been in Louisville since at least May 1810. There is, however, some reason to believe he had been there longer, perhaps even before the fall of 1809. Because Clark and his family were still on their eastern trip in May 1810, and because it would have been difficult for him to make the necessary arrangements for York while he was traveling, the chances are good that York had been sent to Louisville before the trip began in September 1809. Also, the fact that the slave Scot, not York, attended Clark throughout this trip seems to support the view that by September 1809 York was no longer a member of the Clark household in St. Louis. But even though these conjectures seem reasonable, they are conjectures nonetheless. All there is to be known with certainty is that on Clark's trip, during which he learned of the violent death of Meriwether Lewis, York was somewhere else.[18]

Clark's motive for sending York to Louisville does not appear to have been quite as simple as young O'Fallon makes it sound. According to his understanding of the situation, it was solely so "he might be with his wife," not that his misconduct had played a part in the decision. But this is hard to accept at face value. Had Clark's only purpose been to reunite York with his wife, he could have made other arrangements. He could have sent him to live with any of a number of members of the Clark family residing in or near Louisville, who would have taken better care of him and given him more time off to see his wife than could be expected of any employer. Instead, Clark allowed York to be exposed to a system widely known for its frequent abuse of slaves.

As Professor Kenneth Stampp has written, "The overworking of hired slaves by employers with only a temporary interest in their welfare was as notorious as the harsh practices of overseers," a point he subsequently underscored by adding that the "hired slave stood the greatest chance of subjection to cruel punishments as well as overwork."[19] Whether York was similarly mistreated by Mr. Young, except for having been poorly clothed, it is impossible to say, although a man who would keep a slave in tatters would not have been likely to treat him kindly in other ways. But it is Clark's behavior, not Young's, which is most perplexing. Because he must have known that the interest of employers in their hired slaves was entirely economic, unmitigated by any emotional ties or personal concerns for their well-being, why did he take the definite risk that his longtime companion, body servant, and fellow member of the expedition might be callously used?

Unless Clark had some form of punishment in mind, his decision to have York hired out is inexplicable. This is by no means to imply that he expected York to be abused, for everything known of Clark as a man says he was not vindictive. Rather, his feelings at the time appear to have been a mixture of anger and compassion: anger to the extent of banishing York from St. Louis and having him hired out, yet leavened with enough compassion to allow him to be near his wife in Louisville. It may even have been that he wanted York to be lowered in status only temporarily, with it his intention to assign him to one of the Louisville Clarks later. But this is only a speculation, just as it is only a speculation to observe that when Clark learned of York's plight he seems to have been uncomfortable with what he had permitted to happen. At least he thereafter avoided making any mention of either their falling out or of York's mistreatment at the hands of Mr. Young. From what he told Nicholas Biddle, Washington Irving, and William Clark Kennerly, the impression was given that nothing had ever come between them. But speculations are not substitutes for facts, and since all knowledge of the matter begins and ends with O'Fallon's letter, this strange episode in the lives of Clark and York remains an enigma.

Of York's marriage, neither his wife's name nor the year in which they were wed is known. Owned by a family living in Louisville, she probably became his wife on one of the trips he and Clark made to visit relatives there in the years following the expedition's return. (In view of Lewis having specified in his letter to Clark that their recruits be single men, it is doubtful York was married before the expedition began.)[20] If the wedding ceremony followed the customary ritual for household slaves, the bride and groom would have been married at the home of one of the masters, would have feasted sumptuously, and, as part of the post-nuptial revelries, would have jumped over a broomstick to determine who would "wear the pants" in the family.[21] Also, if the ceremony followed custom, the words of the service itself probably included the phrase "until death or *distance* do you part," a variation on the standard service often inserted and stressed by slave preachers as a grim reminder of how impermanent these unions could be.[22] Unrecognized by law, slave marriages were often torn apart when masters had to pay off debts, when estates had to be settled, or, as was about to happen to York, when the family owning one of the partners moved away. With his wife's owner about to take her to Natchez, York's chances of seeing her again were slim. Not only were slaves restricted from traveling on their own, but even a freed slave, which York would one day become, would have been loath to start life anew in Mississippi, a part of the Deep South all blacks viewed with apprehension. Having lost the good opinion of his master, having been cast down from the high position of a body servant to one of the meanest of all slave stations, and now about to have his wife taken from him by a circumstance against which he was powerless to protest, York's life had surely reached its lowest ebb.

Because of the two men's long association, it is natural to want to think O'Fallon's letter so moved Clark that he forgave York and granted him freedom at this time. And perhaps he did, for with York having repented of whatever he had done and his wife soon to be taken from Louisville, there would have been no reason to keep him either in his wretched frame of mind or in Louisville any longer. Putting wishful thinking to the side, however, the existing evidence simply does not warrant the conclusion that Clark freed York in 1811 and "was ever afterwards interested in his welfare," a conclusion reached by one writer as the result of a misinterpretation of O'Fallon's letter.[23] Actually, the only source ever to state that York was freed is Washington Irving in the notes he made of his conversation with Clark in 1832. Even then, when Irving informs us that at some unspecified point in time York had been granted his freedom, we are left to wonder whether he and Clark were ever reconciled.

13. York's Freedom, Failure, and Reported Death

In 1832, when Washington Irving returned to the United States from having lived in Europe for seventeen years, he reacquainted himself with his native land by traveling west and taking a tour of the prairies. On September 13, while passing through St. Louis, he rode out of the city to William Clark's country home and spent part of the day with him, in the course of which the two men talked about various subjects, including York. How he came into the conversation is not clear, but it is fortunate he did, for the following notes Irving made of what he was told have turned out to be the principal source of information about York's release from slavery and life as a free man.

> His slaves—set them free—one he placed at a ferry—another on a farm, giving him land, horses, &c.—a third he gave a large waggon & team of 6 horses to ply between Nashville and Richmond. They all repented & wanted to come back.
>
> The waggoner was York, the hero of the Missouri expedition & adviser of the Indians. He could not get up early enough in the morng—his horses were ill kept—two died—the others grew poor. He sold them, was cheated—entered into service—fared ill. ["]Damn this freedom,["] said York, ["]I have never had a happy day since I got it.["] He determined to go back to his old master—set off for St Louis, but was taken with the cholera in Tennessee & died. Some of the traders think they have met traces of York's crowd, on the Missouri.[1]

Irving's words seem to say all there is to be said about York's inability to cope with freedom. He was so lazy he could not run his drayage business properly; he was so gullible he was cheated when he sold his remaining horses; and, after having fared badly in domestic service, he was so in need of a master to take care of him that he was returning to Clark when he was stricken with cholera and died. Perhaps this is exactly what happened and York brought all his troubles on himself. At least Clark seems to have had

Portrait of Washington Irving, who visited William Clark in 1832. Clark told him York had been freed, had failed in a drayage business, and had died of cholera in Tennessee while trying to return "to his old master." There are some, however, who think York instead lived on, went back to the Rockies, and became a member of the Crow tribe. *Rare Books and Manuscripts Division, The New York Public Library, Astor, Lenox and Tilden Foundations.*

no doubts this had been the case, although, with him living in St. Louis and York driving his wagon between Nashville and Richmond, he almost surely was reporting only what he had been told, not what he had witnessed for himself.[2] But even if it is assumed that Clark's account of what had befallen York is essentially accurate, it can be interpreted in two entirely different ways: from the point of view of the master and from the point of view of the former slave. When this is done, some questions arise as to what Clark's feelings about York really were. Some questions also arise as to whether the causes of York's failure were quite as simple as Clark made them sound.

The opening words of the notes, "His slaves—set them free," convey the impression that Clark had freed all his slaves, but it is unclear whether Irving believed this or was merely referring to the three to whom he had given a ferry, a farm, and a drayage business. Regardless, Clark had not freed all his slaves, nor would he do so by the time of his death in 1838.[3] As for York, Clark obviously felt he had received a golden opportunity, both in terms of freedom and a business, only to fail miserably—so miserably that he had

Cieul - Clarks old house . mo .

William Clark's country home outside St. Louis, where Washington Irving called on him. *Missouri Historical Society.*

decided to relinquish his freedom and resume his former servile status. Irving's words also leave little question that Clark spoke sardonically of York, particularly in the references to him having been "the hero of the Missouri expedition" and to traders on the Missouri thinking they had "met traces of York's crowd." Over the years, both of these statements have been interpreted to York's discredit. The first has been taken literally to mean he brashly boasted of having been a leading figure of the expedition, although Clark was probably merely alluding to his penchant for telling preposterous tales, not criticizing him for having overstepped his bounds. The second has been taken to mean that York fathered a horde of children while in the West, an assumption totally unsupported by the journals kept at the time. Yet, despite the words about York fathering children having been blown out of all proportion as time went on, it is strange Clark even discussed the matter with his distinguished visitor. To all appearances offered as a conversational tidbit, the reference to traders having detected traces of York's blood among the natives distinctly implies that it was somehow amusing for a black man to have had sexual relations with Indian women.

It also leaves out the rest of the story. As Clark was well aware, York was not the only member of the expedition to have done so.

The unflattering portrait Clark painted of the man who had long been his body servant and had accompanied him on the historic crossing of the continent is perplexing. In trying to understand why Clark spoke as he did, one can only surmise that he had mixed feelings about having granted York freedom, just as other masters who freed their slaves are known to have had mixed feelings about having freed them. In a number of ways, Clark mirrored the enlightened and the conventional thinking of his time. On the one hand, he did free some of his slaves, whereas the vast majority of slaveholders did not, and in the case of Ben, the slave he manumitted in 1802, he declared "perpetual involuntary servitude to be contrary of principles of natural Justice." On the other hand, he evidently attributed York's failure in business entirely to laziness and incompetence, a rather typical white view of blacks which did not take into account the self-evident fact that "slavery was a poor school for freedom."[4] Paradoxically, not only did some masters who freed their slaves have a low opinion of black intelligence and industry, but they also were not wholly displeased when a slave they had freed made a botch of things and asked to be taken back. When this happened—and it happened more often than might be thought—it both enhanced the master's image of himself and provided a needed justification for having owned or still owning slaves.

Those who held black men and women in bondage, as Clark still did, had to believe that slaves were happier and better off under the firm guidance of a master than in trying to wrestle with the problems freedom brought. Quite simply, if they did not believe this, then any moral grounds for owning a single slave would have vanished instantly from underfoot. While on the surface it may appear to be absurdly illogical to say that masters who were humane enough to free their slaves could derive a degree of satisfaction when they did not do well, it must be remembered that slavery was indeed a peculiar institution, requiring whites and blacks alike to go to lengths to rationalize their roles within it. Clark's ambivalence about the slaves he had freed is indicated by the sentence in which the two he had given a ferry and a farm are included with York. Unlike York, no mention is made of them having failed, yet "They all repented & wanted to come

Clark
to
Negro Ben

Know all Men by these presents that I William Clark of Jefferson County and State of Kentucky for and in consideration of the Services already rendered to me by my negro man Slave Ben and regarding perpetual involuntary servitude to be contrary of principles of natural Justice do emancipate & set free forever the said negro man Slave Ben — and I do hereby relinquish all power and Authority over the said Ben as a Slave and do allow him all the Rights, privileges — and advantages of a free man to be enjoyed by him in as ample manner as if he had been born free In Witness whereof I have hereto set my hand and Seal this 10th day of Decr 1802

Exd in presence of
William Clark (Seal)

In this instrument of manumission signed by Clark in 1802, he freed a slave named Ben. York was freed at some time after May 1811, but no official record of his manumission has been found. *Archives and Records Service, Jefferson County, Kentucky.*

back," with the word *repented* sounding as though they had done something wrong in accepting their freedom in the first place. To the extent that Clark believed all three former slaves had come to regret choosing freedom when it was offered, he reacted in a fairly conventional way.

Where Clark was far from conventional was in freeing any slaves at all. In doing so, he boldly went against the grain of public opinon, for most Southern whites were vehemently opposed to manumissions in the belief that free blacks were a dangerously disruptive influence on the slave community, a constant, potentially explosive reminder that it was possible to be both black and free. Although the exact year in which Clark freed York is not known, it certainly was well after large-scale slave uprisings in the Caribbean had sent shock waves through the South. These uprisings, followed by a few small and scattered uprisings by American slaves, created

Black troops hang French soldiers in Santo Domingo. The large-scale slave rebellions which took place in the Caribbean and sent shock waves throughout the South were never duplicated in the United States, although a few small, scattered uprisings did occur. *From M. Rainsford, Black Empire of Hayti, 1805.*

an uneasiness about all blacks best described in these words: "Many men of the South thought of themselves and their neighbors as living above a loaded mine, in which the negro slaves were the powder, the abolitionists the spark, and the free negroes the fuse."[5] Consequently, laws throughout the slave states were written to make the manumission process difficult, such as requiring owners to provide those they freed with the means to make a living—hence, Clark's gift to York of "a large waggon & team of 6 horses"—and in some instances specifying that a former owner's property could be attached if his ex-slaves were unable to support themselves. Because the manumission of a slave was no light matter, either in the eyes of the law or society, Clark must have given much thought to his decision to free York.

There is now no way of knowing how Clark arrived at his decision, but it is obvious the arguments for freeing York finally won out over those for keeping him a slave. Perhaps he belatedly came to the conclusion that York had earned his freedom by serving on the expedition. Perhaps he was swayed by O'Fallon's poignant letter reporting York's mistreatment as a hired slave and the impending loss of his wife. Or perhaps in the end principle alone outweighed whatever reservations he may have had. For his part, York could not have been oblivious of the hardships and indignities he would have to face as a free black. Spurned by whites as social outcasts and forced to compete at the lowest economic level with slave labor, free blacks were far from being free men. Yet, as bleak as the prospects were, York apparently wanted to taste freedom so much that he was willing to take his chances with it. As for the relationship between Clark and York, Clark did not forever harbor resentment for whatever had come between them prior to 1811. Although Irving's notes provide no clue as to whether they ever settled their differences in person, William Clark Kennerly's memories from the 1820s and 1830s of his uncle's fond references to "his faithful York" reveal that Clark had long since ceased to be angry.[6] Nevertheless, as much as one would like to fathom the innermost feelings of these two men whose lives were so intimately connected, it is not possible. By virtue of the color of the skin each was born with, one was a master and the other was a slave, and who today can begin to put himself in either of their places?

If Washington Irving had been able to talk with York about his life as a free black, he undoubtedly would have come away with an entirely different impression than the one given him by Clark. This is by no means to suggest that York was blameless for his failure or to make undue excuses for him, but only to point out that his side of the story has never been considered. Even when it is granted that York must have brought many of his problems on himself, Clark's explanation of his failure as due solely to laziness and ineptitude has to be questioned. After all, York's bitter experience with freedom was common with free blacks, and the reason most of them lived on the ragged edge of poverty cannot be attributed to every one of them having been lazy and inept. (Actually, in view of the overwhelming social and economic odds they were up against, it is remarkable more did not become discouraged to the point of desperation than did.) In order to understand just how difficult York's life must have been, some notice should be taken of the formidable barriers raised against all free blacks in the South, while keeping in mind that with most of them lacking education and job skills they had little reason to believe they could fare much better in the North. And lest it be thought that except for work-related problems the white population above the Mason-Dixon line extended welcoming open arms, the author of a book about free blacks reminds us, "Blatant racism in the North made the free states a forbidding alternative."[7]

When a slave received his freedom, he was given a certificate stating he had legally been freed from bondage and no longer was the property of any man. But these so-called free papers did not make him truly free, because, as he soon discovered, he "generally remained at the bottom of the social order, despised by whites, burdened with increasingly oppressive racial proscriptions, and subjected to verbal and physical abuse."[8] So fearful were most masters that free blacks would make their slaves discontented with their lot, they forbade the two to mingle, and in many places laws prohibiting free blacks from entertaining slaves in their homes were rigidly enforced by the bodily punishment of both free and slave violators.[9] In Tennessee, where York must have spent much time while driving his wagon to and from Nashville, the law called for a free black to be lashed fifteen times on the bare back if found in the company of slaves.[10] Thus, to all intents and purposes, free blacks were ostracized, completely separated from whites and cut off from even their own enslaved people. For York, life could not have been easy. Having left behind all of his black relatives and friends in Louisville and St. Louis, now eyed with suspicion and hostility by whites, and limited entirely to other free blacks for companionship, he would have been hard pressed to build anything resembling a normal social life.

Even though he was legally free and had the papers to prove it, York must have awakened every morning with the nagging fear that before the day was out he could be a slave again. Required by the proscriptive codes to produce his certificate of freedom upon the demand of any suspicious white, he did not dare lose or misplace it, for he could be accused of being a runaway slave, imprisoned, and sold back into slavery. A greater fear, however, was that of being kidnapped. Unscrupulous whites, making a business of selling free blacks back into bondage, roamed in search of victims throughout the South and audaciously made forays into the North as well. Pouncing upon unsuspecting victims, they quickly sold them to slave traders, who usually spirited them off to large plantations in the Deep South, where the chances of them ever being heard of again were small.[11] Fully aware that "in isolated rural areas, at odd hours, kidnappers acted with impunity," York surely approached those days when he had to travel on lonely country roads with more than a touch of apprehension.[12]

Of York's efforts to earn a living, Irving's notes make depressing reading: "He could not get up early enough in the morng—his horses were ill kept—two died—the others grew poor. He sold them, was cheated—entered into service—fared ill." While every one of these statements may have been true, at least to some degree, what is left unsaid is that even if York had been highly motivated to succeed, he would have had a hard time doing so. Having spent almost all of his life as a body servant, he would have been woefully unprepared to run a business, especially one requiring him to compete for jobs, negotiate freighting charges, and keep his finances in order. The probability is also extremely high that he could not read or write and therefore would have been at a disadvantage to any who may have wished to cheat him. Now, in his dealings with whites, there would have been no one to look out for his interests, not even courts of law, for free blacks were denied equal access to them. Nor, as had been the case when he was the famous William Clark's body servant, would he have been spared the usual humiliations inflicted on black people, slave and free alike. A product of a lifetime of slavery, York could only have been confused by all the changes thrust upon him, changes to which he was obviously unable to adjust.

Former slaves soon found themselves struggling not so much to succeed as simply to survive. Except for the few who were fortunate enough to have received special training (tailors, blacksmiths, and the like), most had to offer themselves at the lowest wage level, and even then they were usually passed over in favor of cheaper slave labor. As a result, "Poverty forced many of them to accept whatever pay they were offered, to work at two or three jobs to earn a living, and to send their wives and children out to work to make ends meet."[13] What is more, those who like York were set up with a business had reason to believe that even if they did succeed it might not be for long. From colonial times, whites resented and opposed the participation of free blacks in the better paying forms of employment, causing more and more doors of opportunity to be closed as the years passed.[14] For example, before Clark discussed York with Washington Irving in 1832, whites had already taken over the drayage business from free blacks in Baltimore and New Orleans, and elsewhere in the South poor whites and immigrants moving up the economic ladder had dislodged many from their customary trades.[15]

Irving's notes do not tell us where York worked as a domestic servant after having lost his drayage business, but it probably was in Tennessee, where he is reported to have died of cholera while on his way to St. Louis. Although the words "fared ill" with regard to his domestic service can be interpreted to mean that he either proved unsatisfactory in the performance of his duties or was not treated well by his employer, one would think his long experience as a body servant would have more than adequately prepared him for household tasks. Nothing is said about how long he remained a servant, but it must have been for at least a year and could have been longer. The standard practice of employers who hired free blacks was to bind them to contracts for a year's time, a period often too short to accumulate enough money to do anything but renew their contracts for one or more terms.[16] By and large, these contracts "specified that the free Negroes work according to the rules governing field hands," and in most instances they were observed to the letter, with no distinctions made between blacks who were free and blacks who were property.[17] Under these conditions, York probably found himself to be no better off—and perhaps much worse off—than he had been as a slave.

Having failed in business, having been cheated when he sold his four remaining horses, and having fallen back into the equivalent of bondage, it is not surprising that York exclaimed: "Damn this freedom. I have never had a happy day since I got it." It is also not surprising that he then set out to return to Clark in St. Louis. Trapped within a system where they were unwanted and seldom allowed to scrape out more than a bare living, many free blacks ultimately had no choice but to retreat to relatively secure lives under the protection of former masters.[18] Slavery, as they conclusively demonstrated, was indeed a poor school for freedom. On no less than two counts, they were tragically ill-equipped to deal with the hard realities of the world into which they had been released: they lacked the basic skills needed to avoid poverty, and, as two psychiatrists have tellingly observed, slavery by its very nature molded the black man into "a psychologically emasculated and totally dependent human being."[19] York seems to have been no exception.

According to Washington Irving, York never made it back to Clark, "but was taken with the cholera in Tennessee & died," with those stark words evoking the picture of a defeated man in the last throes of a terrible disease far from friends and family. As much as one would like to think he deserved better for having once served both his master and his country well, the fates were evidently less than kind at the end. (Unless one chooses to believe the fascinating story, to be examined in the next chapter, that he lived on and managed to find his way to happiness and respect among the Crow Indians in the Rocky Mountains.) Unfortunately, Irving's notes are silent as to when York was freed and when he died, and so too are all manumission and death records in Kentucky, Missouri, and Tennessee, the first two of those states being by far the most probable places for him to have been freed.[20] Nevertheless, when the laws and practices pertaining to the manumission of slaves are applied to what is known about York, it appears that he could not have been freed later than 1815. On the other hand, it is much more difficult to estimate when he may have died.

One of the documents to be considered when trying to place York's whereabouts between the time of O'Fallon's letter in 1811 and Clark's conversation with Irving in 1832 does not even mention his name. On the front cover of a cash book and journal Clark kept for the years 1825–1828, he listed the names of all the members of the expedition, except York's, along with remarks as to whether they were then living or dead.[21] Although his omission of York's name cannot be explained, two reasons rule out that it was because York was still his slave and simply taken for granted. Mary Kennerly Taylor, who was born in 1818, later vividly recalled the names of a number of slaves who were prominent members of the Clark household when she was growing up in St. Louis.[22] Since York was

Although faded and barely discernible, the names written on the cover of a cash book and journal Clark kept from 1825–1828 include all the members of the expedition except York. There is no satisfactory explanation as to why Clark left him out when he listed the other members along with remarks as to whether they were then living or dead. *Courtesy of the Everett D. Graff Collection, The Newberry Library, Chicago.*

not among them, and since she surely would have mentioned him had he still been her Uncle William's slave, he must have been gone by the time her memories were formed, or by the mid-1820s. Secondly, manumission laws and practices in Missouri and Kentucky make it all but certain York had been freed well before the 1820s, despite the statement by William Clark Kennerly that when Julia Clark's health began to fail in 1819 Clark took her to the mountains of Virginia with York along "to look after his master."[23] As always, it is not easy to separate the wheat from the chaff where Kennerly's memories are concerned, but in this instance he has to have been wrong. From everything known, York would have been in his mid-forties in 1819, an age much too old for Clark thereafter to have released him from slavery and sent him out into the world on his own.

Because a body servant was almost always chosen from among his young master's playmates, and because Clark reminisced of his "little Negro boy, York" from their childhoods in Virginia, York was probably born no more than five years after Clark, or by 1775. This would have put him in his mid-thirties in 1811, when O'Fallon's letter tells us he was still a slave in Louisville. Perhaps the letter persuaded Clark to set York free at that time, although nothing is known of his reaction to O'Fallon's words. However, no matter what his reaction may have been, the manumission laws and practices of Missouri and Kentucky would have forced him to act by no later than 1815. In Missouri, the law explicitly stated that slaves could not be freed if they were more than forty years of age, and York should have been at least forty in 1815.[24] While Kentucky laid down no specific age limit, the law stipulated that "a manumitted slave must not become a burden to the public because of age or infirmity," thereby reflecting the general conviction that older slaves could not support themselves.[25] Bearing in mind that slaves of fifty were thought to be old and that slaves of more than forty were seldom freed, Clark would surely not have waited until York was in his forties to have freed him.

While there are good reasons to think York was freed between 1811 and 1815, there is practically no information to go on in trying to estimate when he may have died. (Indeed, the information is so sparse one historian gave credence to a mistaken obituary having him living until 1878 and freezing to death in, of all places, Virginia.)[26] Although it can be assumed that York spent at least the customary one-year term in domestic service, Irving's notes give no inkling of how long he had his drayage business. But if he had been as lazy and inept as Irving's notes say he was, he probably would have failed sooner than later, with it not unlikely that he lost the business within just two or three years. If so, he could have lived for as few as three or four years after becoming a free man, and, depending upon the year in which he was freed, he could have died as early as 1814 or as late as 1819. This is, however, nothing more than a guess. All there is to be said with certainty is that by 1832 Clark had heard that his former body servant was dead.

But did York, having experienced one misfortune after another, as well as having suffered the usual indignities inflicted on all free blacks, really set out to return to Clark and die of cholera in Tennessee? Or did he instead decide to seek a new life in a place and among a people where he would be both truly free and welcomed? In an extraordinary story which has largely been dismissed as too incredible to be true, a trapper in the Rocky Mountains in the early 1830s met an old black man living among the Crows who told him he had traveled to the Pacific with Lewis and Clark, had returned with them, and had subsequently gone back to the West. Could he have been York? The odds against it would appear to be very large, to say the least. And yet, when the old black man's story is examined closely, it cannot be ripped to shreds. In fact, for those who wish to believe the man was York, a sizeable body of evidence strongly contradicts all previous identifications of him as having been someone else.

IV

THE STRANGEST
STORY OF ALL

14. Did York Live On and Return to the West?

In November of 1832, a young man named Zenas Leonard was a member of a group of mountain men who had traveled far beyond the frontier to trap the rivers and streams of the Rocky Mountains. Five of their horses having been stolen by Crows, the trappers followed the Indians to their village in north-central Wyoming, where they met a black man who was living with the tribe. On the advice of this "old Negro," as Leonard would describe him, the trappers gave the Crows a few trinkets, recovered their horses peacefully, and eventually went on their way, but not before the man had told them a remarkable story Leonard later recounted in these words:

> In this village we found a Negro man, who informed us that he first came to this country with Lewis and Clark—with whom he also returned to the state of Missouri, and in a few years returned again with a Mr. Mac-kinney, a trader on the Missouri river, and has remained here ever since—which is about ten or twelve years. He has acquired a correct knowledge of their manner of living, and speaks their language fluently. He has rose to be quite a considerable character, or chief, in their village; at least he assumes all the dignities of a chief, for he has four wives with whom he lives alternately. This is the custom of many of the chiefs.[1]

Two years later, after having gone to California and back with Joseph Walker's company of trappers, Leonard met the same Crows and saw the same black man again. Of this second meeting in the fall of 1834, he wrote in a narrative of his adventures that he found the man to be as helpful as he had been before, and he restated what he had written earlier about the man's ability to speak Crow fluently, his familiarity with tribal customs, and his high standing in the village. Then, in a sentence one cannot refrain from contrasting with Washington Irving's description of York's unhappiness and failure as a free black, Leonard added, "He enjoys perfect peace and satisfaction, and has everything that he desires at his own command."[2] With winter approaching, Joseph Walker and his main body of trappers departed to build sheltered quarters elsewhere, leaving Leonard and two other men to reside with the Crows "for the purpose of instigating them in the business of catching beaver and buffalo."[3] Soon after this, Leonard witnessed a bloody battle in which the black man turned the tide.

Near the end of November 1834, sixty-nine Blackfeet warriors invaded the traditional hunting grounds of the Crows, but were quickly forced to barricade themselves behind a breastwork of rocks and brush on the brow of a hill. Despite being greatly outnumbered, the Blackfeet repeatedly repulsed the attacking Crows until, in Leonard's words, "confusion spread through their ranks—many appeared overwhelmed with despair—and the whole Crow nation was about to retreat from the field."[4] At this point, the black man stepped forward and harangued his fellow tribesmen as cowards who were acting more like squaws than braves and who would make themselves the laughingstock of whites and Indians alike if they did not drive off these arrogant invaders. As Leonard pictured the scene, the black man first worked the Crows into a frenzy, then led the assault himself.

> The old Negro continued in this strain until they became greatly animated, and told them that if the red man was afraid to go among his enemy, he would show them that a black man was not, and he leaped from the rock on which he had been standing, and looking neither to the right nor to the left, made for the fort as fast as he could run. The Indians guessing his purpose, and inspired by his words and fearless example, followed close to his heels, and were in the fort dealing destruction to the right and left nearly as soon as the old man.[5]

The battle turned into a massacre, all the Blackfeet were slain, and the Crows began the rituals of celebrating their victory and mourning their dead. The "old Negro" was not killed or even wounded, for, as Leonard wrote, "The person who struck the first blow at their late battle with the Blackfeet now commenced dancing and was immediately followed by every young man and woman belonging to the tribe (except the mourners, who stood silent, melancholy spectators)."[6] After this, the man is never mentioned again. He completely vanishes from Leonard's narrative, leaving many questions unanswered, just as York does from Washington Irving's brief and equally tantalizing account of his conversation with William Clark.

Who was this man who said he had gone to the Pacific with Lewis and Clark and was found to be living a stranger-than-fiction life among the Crows? Surprisingly, the question has never been given much attention, with the few who have ventured an answer usually doing so only in short footnotes or in passing comments in their texts. What is more, although only three men have ever been named as possibilities, the arguments for and against them have never been examined side by side, nor have the arguments been reviewed in recent years in light of new and sometimes contradictory information. Consequently, judgments made long ago may no longer be valid. For example, H.M. Chittenden, the noted turn-of-the-century historian of the fur trade, declared without qualification the man to have been Edward Rose, a trapper of mixed blood who is known to have lived with the Crows, but Chittenden was unaware of a letter written in 1833 which refutes him.[7] Over the years, a number of writers have assumed that the man was James Beckwourth, another trapper of mixed blood who lived with the Crows and actually claimed to have led the attack on the Blackfeet, but they seem to have overlooked the glaring discrepancies in his story. And Reuben Thwaites, the editor of *Original Journals of the Lewis and Clark Expedition*, cast a tentative vote for the man having been York, but he evidently did not know of Irving's conversation with Clark in which York was reported to have died of cholera in Tennessee.[8] With so much confusion surrounding the subject, it appears to be time to weigh the cases for and against Rose, Beckwourth, and York in terms of all the evidence now known to exist.

At first glance, Edward Rose is an excellent prospect. Born at an unknown date of a white father and a mother who was half black and half Cherokee, he traveled up the Missouri to the Bighorn River with Manuel Lisa's trapping and trading expedition of 1807, and soon left it to live with the Crows.[9] This would be in keeping with the first of Zenas Leonard's two conflicting references to when the black man joined the Crows— "a few years" after the return of Lewis and Clark. Rose lived off and on with the Crows until perhaps as late as 1820, is known to have visited them on two occasions after that, and is reported to have been highly regarded by the tribe.[10] Two other reasons also support those who have named him as the man Leonard met: his reputation for ferocity in combat matches the description of the man who fearlessly led the storming of the Blackfoot strong-hold, and he undoubtedly had been told about York by one or more of the many men he was acquainted with who had either been on the expedition or had intimate knowledge of it. While with Manuel Lisa, he associated with George Drouillard, John Colter, John Potts, and Peter Wiser, all formerly with Lewis and Clark; he later was involved with Toussaint Charbonneau in a shady scheme to buy and sell Indian women; and for a time he trapped for Reuben Lewis, Meriwether's brother.[11] Nevertheless, as strong as to all appearances the case is for Rose having been Leonard's "old Negro," it is demolished by a letter which seems not to have come to the attention of scholars until the late 1930s.

Dated 26 July 1833, a year and four months before Zenas Leonard was present at the battle between the Crows and the Blackfeet, this letter from an Indian agent who had recently returned from the Upper Missouri reported Edward Rose to be dead. Writing to William Clark, then Superintendent of Indian Affairs, John F. A. Sanford described the murders of Rose and two other mountain men by Arikara Indians in the winter of 1832-1833 as follows:

> During the last winter a war party belonging to that nation came on the Yellowstone below the Big Horn where they fell in with three men belonging to A. [American] Fur Co. who they treacherously killed....They scalped them and left part of the scalps of each tied to poles on the grounds of the murder. A large party of Crows went in pursuit of them the same evening or next day but could not overtake them. The names of the men killed are Rose, Menard & Glass.[12]

Rose was dead, without question, and so were Menard and Glass. In fact, James Beckwourth himself claimed to have identified the bodies, and Johnson Gardner, a veteran trapper, gave the touring Prince Maximilian of Wied an account of the murders and of how he and several other trappers had avenged them.[13] Nor do modern-day students of the fur trade doubt that the three men were killed during the winter of 1832-1833. Where some doubt has been cast is on Leonard's accuracy in dating the Crow battle with the Blackfeet as having taken place in 1834. Plagued with the problem of the black man's identity and unable to accept either Beckwourth or York as an alternate possibility, those who have continued to in-

Mountain man James Beckwourth was fifty-seven years old in 1855. This daguerreotype was
made of him about that time. Some think he was the "old Negro" member of the Crow tribe who
in 1832 told Zenas Leonard that he had been to the Pacific with Lewis and Clark. However, both
his age and his appearance make it most unlikely that he was the man. *Nevada Historical Society.*

sist that he was Rose—even when they were aware of Sanford's letter—
have engaged in mental gymnastics. At the same time they have relied on
Leonard as their sole source for saying that Rose was living with the Crows
at the time of the battle, they have maintained that his memory must have
been faulty by two years, with the battle having had to occur before Rose
was killed in the winter of 1832-1833.[14] But this argument does not hold
water.

With regard to Leonard's reliability as a reporter, he has been called an
outstanding exception among members of the fur trade "in that he not only
wrote down his experiences and observations during the more than four

years that he was in the Rockies and beyond, but he also published them within five years of his return from the mountains."[15] While it is said part of his journal was stolen by Indians, which would have required him to fill in the balance from memory, he was in the West such a short time—only from the spring of 1831 until the summer of 1835—it is inconceivable that his dating of the Crow-Blackfoot battle could be off by two years. Moreover, between his first meeting with the black man late in 1832 and his report of the battle in 1834, he spent a full year with Joseph Walker on his historic overland journey to and from the Spanish settlements in California. If nothing else, this unforgettable experience would have provided such a clear-cut demarcation in time that it is unreasonable to think he would have been unable to recall whether the battle took place before or after it. In short, every available piece of evidence points to the battle having been fought when Leonard says it was, in 1834, or well after Edward Rose was dead.

Could the person Leonard met have been James Beckwourth, one of the most colorful and controversial characters among all the mountain men? Many have thought so for a number of seemingly good reasons. Also of mixed blood (his father was white and his mother a black, a mulatto, or a quadroon), Beckwourth lived with the Crows much of the time between 1829 and 1836, and he often boasted that he had been a war chief of the tribe. As one notorious for "just plain lying for the sake of a good story," as well as adopting the heroic exploits of others as his own, it would have been completely in character for him to have claimed to have been with Lewis and Clark.[16] It is also true that for a period of time he was employed by Kenneth McKenzie, the "Mr. Mackinney" of Leonard's narrative, although, unlike what the black man said about having gone up the Missouri with McKenzie in the 1820s, Beckwourth definitely did not travel with him.[17] Finally, he related to his earliest biographer in self-glorifying detail how he led the Crows in their attack on the Blackfoot barricade. Taken as a whole, the case for Beckwourth is impressive, but upon close examination it contains serious flaws. One which all but rules him out as the "old Negro" Leonard first met in 1832 is that Beckwourth himself tells us he was born in 1798, which would have made him only thirty-four years old by then.

At thirty-four, Beckwourth was just eleven years older than Leonard, who was twenty-three in 1832. It therefore stretches credulity beyond acceptable limits to think that Leonard would have described him as old not just once but twice—first as an "old Negro," then as an "old man." At the same time, it is impossible to believe that Leonard would not have seen instantly that Beckwourth was much too young to have been with Lewis and Clark over a quarter of a century earlier. And should some say these statements about his youthful appearance are only assumptions and he could have looked much older than his years, a daguerreotype made of him in about 1855, when he was fifty-seven, negates that as a possibility. Made more than twenty years after Leonard met the man he called an "old Negro," the daguerreotype reveals Beckwourth to have looked far from old even then: his hair was coal black, his face was relatively unlined, and he still had the bearing of a vigorous man.

The daguerreotype is revealing on another count. While it shows Beckwourth to have had a swarthy complexion, as might be expected of a man who had lived outdoors most of his life, it does not show him to have had noticeably negroid features, an observation confirmed by several men who knew him in the flesh. One said there was nothing about his looks to indicate black ancestry, and at least two others who described him seem not to have realized he was of mixed blood.[18] It is also interesting to note that, as far as is known, Beckwourth never used the word *black* in referring to himself. Yet, when the man Leonard knew exhorted the Crows to do battle, he "told them that if the red man was afraid to go among his enemy, he would show them that a black man was not." On the basis of both age and appearance, the case for Beckwourth having been Leonard's "old Negro" simply does not stand up.

Although many have accepted as true Beckwourth's claim of having led the Crows to victory over the Blackfeet, his story shows every sign of being another instance of when he related as his own the deeds of others. In his account of the battle, he said a trapper named Robert Meldrum took part and was injured, but Meldrum, who lived with the Crows at the same time as Beckwourth, did not back him up. Declaring Beckwourth to have been "a humbug" and denying that he ever had much influence with the tribe (as did the man Leonard met), Meldrum belittled Beckwourth's selfheroizing tales of bravery by caustically commenting, "He never distinguished himself in fights."[19]

There is still another reason to reject Beckwourth's claim that he was the hero of the battle. When his account of it is compared with Leonard's, it is as though two entirely different events are being described. Beckwourth says the battle took place in the spring, whereas Leonard dates it in late November. Beckwourth says 160 Blackfeet were killed, whereas Leonard puts the toll at 69. Most significantly, Beckwourth says some 20 trappers fought on the side of the Crows, whereas Leonard mentions none, having explained that all of the trappers except for himself and two others had gone off to establish winter quarters elsewhere.[20] What makes Beckwourth's version extremely suspect is that no one other than he and Leonard ever said he had observed the battle or participated in it, and surely if 20 trappers had fought on the side of the Crows, at least one of them would have told the story at some time.

With Rose out of the picture and a very long shadow of doubt cast over Beckwourth, could the man who said he had been to the Pacific with Lewis and Clark have been York? Although stranger things have happened, the odds against it are enormous. The report of his death in Tennessee would have had to have been a mistake; he would have had to travel a long distance without being recognized or revealing his identity to someone (and the man Leonard met was not reticent about saying he had been with Lewis and Clark); and he would have had to live with the Crows for years without his fascinating story having been heard and passed along by other men of the fur trade than Leonard. But if not York, who was he? Only a guess can be made that he was an unknown black trapper who was living with the Crows and, for motives known only to himself, wanted people to think he had taken part in the exploration.[21] However, this explanation is lame at best, little more than an attempt to explain the unexplainable.

Those who wish to believe that York somehow lived on to enjoy "all the dignities of a chief," including four wives, have every right to do so. Certainly, Leonard's chronology cannot be used to deny them the pleasure of thinking he did not meet his end dejected and alone in Tennessee, but instead found his way to a people who looked upon his blackness as a blessing, not a stigma. If the man Leonard met had joined the Crows "about ten or twelve years" before 1832, as he said he had, this would have been at approximately the time one conjecture made earlier has York disheartened by his failure in business and domestic service. If the conjecture about York's age is roughly correct, he would have been in his late fifties in 1832, or far enough along in years to have been an old man in young Zenas Leonard's eyes. And if Clark's hearsay report of York having died of cholera in Tennessee was in error, he could have made his way back up the Missouri to the country he had crossed years before. But to conclude from all this that the man was York would be carrying conjectures much too far. From what is known, only three things can be stated with confidence: there is no hard evidence that York was dead by 1832, Edward Rose had been killed by the time of the battle with the Blackfeet, and all previous identifications of the man as having been James Beckwourth can be strongly challenged. Beyond this, as is so often the case with York, the trail vanishes before the truth can be reached.

V

THE END OF
THE SEARCH

15. Summing Up

The search for York comes to an end with his death, whether it occurred in Tennessee or, as some would like to believe, years later among the Crows. But while speculations as to when and where he died are interesting, it is more to the point to ask just how much the search has revealed about his life. To this the answer must be that it is less than might be wished and more than might be expected. On the one hand, even after many of the myths and the distortions rooted in prejudice have been exposed for what they are worth, and even after an attempt has been made to understand how slavery shaped him as a person, York can be seen only in a half-light, a man about whom many questions remain unanswered. On the other hand, to be able to piece together so many events in the life of a slave who was born in the 1700s and was unable to leave behind any written record about himself is surprising.[1]

From documents written while or soon after York lived, we know he was the son of two slaves called Rose and "old York"; grew to be an unusually large and powerful man who was "black as a bear"; was inherited by William Clark from his father in 1799; went to the Pacific with his master and Meriwether Lewis on their exploration of the western two-thirds of North America in 1804-1806; was viewed with awe as "big medicine" by Indians who had never seen a black man; proved to be instrumental in keeping the Shoshonis from departing with the horses needed for the expedition to cross the Rockies; returned to civilization and continued to perform his duties as a body servant until at least the time of Clark's marriage in 1808; had a falling out with Clark prior to 1811 and was hired to a man in Louisville who treated him shabbily; in all probability lost his wife when her master moved to Natchez; was eventually freed and given a wagon and six horses, only to learn that freedom brought neither prosperity nor happiness; and died somewhere far from the relatives and friends he had been close to most of his life.

From what was written and said about York by those who knew him, he had his full share of human foibles and admirable traits. When freed and on his own, he is reported to have been so lazy he could not get up in the morning, so careless with his horses that two of them died, and such a total failure in business and domestic service that he decided to give up his freedom and return to his former master. He also at one point did something which must have been shocking in Clark's eyes, for it was an all but unheard-of act for a master to reduce his body servant to the lowly state of a hired slave. On the other side of the coin, York was a kind man, as is testified to by the care he gave the dying Sergeant Floyd. He was a man of sufficient intelligence and polish to be a body servant, a position at the very top of the slave hierarchy. He was a man whose loyalty led him to search for Clark at risk to himself during the violent storm at the Great Falls. He was a man with a sense of humor, as well as a talent for drawing a long bow. And he was a man whose courage his comrades who kept journals on the expedition never once questioned.

It is ironic that although not a single derogatory remark was made about York in any of the journals of the Lewis and Clark Expedition, most of what has been written about him since has been tainted with prejudice. Time and again, he has been depicted as a jolly, irresponsible "darkie" whose only contribution to the enterprise was to make his companions laugh. In this regard, York is a classic example of the way American history was for so long written from an almost exclusively white point of view, with blacks more often than not presented as stereotypes of the ridiculous kind found in minstrel shows. But the real York, the York who continues to elude us, was no simple stereotype. As a living, breathing man, he was as complex and full of contradictions as any other. As a man who endured the degradation and despair of slavery, he had thoughts and feelings which today cannot even be imagined. And as a man who was among the first to go beyond the sunset to the end of the continent, he knew the rare satisfaction of having done what no one had ever done before. For him to continue to be thought of as a racial stereotype would be, to put it mildly, a sad perversion of both history and common decency.

From the time he was a slave boy until he died in Tennessee (or just possibly among the Crows), York's life touched the heights and the depths of the world in which he lived. He served and was intimately associated with two men whose names rank high among all explorers; he knew one of the giants of the American Revolution, George Rogers Clark; he was for many months the daily companion of Sacagawea, one of this country's most honored women; and in all likelihood he met the man who dreamed of and designed the expedition, Thomas Jefferson. He saw with his own eyes whole new horizons of prairies, plains, and gigantic snow-capped mountains, and he shared the exultation expressed for all by his master when the expedition's objective was at last reached: "*Ocian in view*! O! the joy." At the same time, he knew what it was like to be the personal property of another man, to have a market value placed upon his body, to be helpless to prevent his wife from being taken from him, and to be despised because of his blackness even after he was legally free.[2] In many different ways, the best and the worst York's world had to offer was reflected in his life.

On 15 January 1807, Meriwether Lewis sent Henry Dearborn, the Secretary of War, a roster of the men who had served with the expedition. In his closing remarks, he wrote:

> With rispect to all those persons whose names are entered on this roll, I feel a peculiar pleasure in declaring, that the Ample support which they gave me under every difficulty; the manly firmness which they evinced on every necessary occasion; and the patience and fortitude with which they submitted to, and bore, the fatigues and painful sufferings incident to my late tour to the Pacific Ocean, entitles them to my warmest approbation and thanks; nor will I suppress the expression of a hope, that the recollection of services thus faithfully performed will meet a just reward in an ample remuneration on the part of our Government.[3]

Perhaps by oversight, perhaps because he was not formally a member of the military contingent, or perhaps because he was a slave and therefore beneath official notice, York's name is missing from Lewis's roster. For him there was neither approbation nor thanks for services faithfully performed, and no request for "a just reward in an ample remuneration on the part of our Government."[4] As far as the public record goes—and as far as most Americans now know—it is as though he had never been along, had never been one of those resourceful and determined few who led the way west across a largely unknown landscape which in time would be shown on maps as the states of Illinois, Missouri, Kansas, Nebraska, Iowa, South Dakota, North Dakota, Montana, Idaho, Washington, and Oregon.

It is, of course, too late to make amends to York for not having received a just reward within his lifetime and for having been maligned for so long after his death. But it is perhaps not too late to pay a debt long overdue by giving him what he surely deserves, yet for almost two centuries has been denied: simple respect and understanding as a human being, as well as a measure of recognition for having played a part in shaping the destiny of this land.

Acknowledgments

In addition to the institutions and government agencies named at the beginning of the bibliography, thanks are due the many people who helped me with this book. Some led me to documents I did not know existed; some gave valuable scholarly advice; some checked archives for pertinent materials in places I was unable to visit; some listened to me think out loud and asked challenging questions; some assisted with the many tedious chores associated with any manuscript; and some simply offered encouragement when it was most needed. Without trying to describe the contributions made by each, I thank them all for cheerfully and generously lending a hand during the search for York—Irving W. Anderson, Beverly D. Bishop, Marshall R. Bristow, Philip J. Canfield, Dr. Eldon G. Chuinard, Paul R. Cutright, Jack Grossman, Lewis and Shirley Krohn, Robert E. Lange, James H. Marshall, Joan M. Morcerf, John H. Peace, William J. Peace, William P. Sherman, Frances H. Stadler, Henry Surval, Samuel W. Thomas, Ahlert D. Wolff, and Janice Worden.

Special thanks are reserved for my wife. Without her steady and enthusiastic support, the book could not (in the words so often used by the journalists of the Lewis and Clark Expedition) have "proceeded on."

Notes

In sentences containing more than one statement or quotation to be documented, sources are cited in the order in which the statements or quotations appear.

Preface

1. Donald Jackson, ed., *Letters of the Lewis and Clark Expedition with Related Documents, 1783-1854*, 1:13.
2. Ibid.
3. Ibid., 1:4.
4. The land embraced by the Louisiana Purchase was vaguely delineated because only its eastern fringes had been explored, but it was generally thought to include the western half of the Mississippi's drainage basin from that river's source in the north to the Red River in the South, and to extend as far west as to "the height of land" known today as the Continental Divide. (Marshall Sprague, *So Vast So Beautiful a Land*, pp. xvii-xviii.)
5. Bernard DeVoto, ed., *The Journals of Lewis and Clark*, p. lii.
6. Private John Potts had come from Germany and enlisted in the army before signing on with Lewis and Clark. While the correct spelling of the Indian girl's name has long been the subject of scholarly debate, most present-day authorities on the expedition concur with the United States Bureau of Ethnology that it should be Sacagawea, not Sacajawea. (See Irving W. Anderson, "Sacajawea, Sacagawea, Sakakawea?")
7. Some slaves were now and then known by their masters' surnames, but this was simply a matter of convenience, not law. Actually, a slave was permitted to own nothing, not even the clothes on his back, for the right of ownership "gave the presumption of a free status." (Harrison A. Trexler, "Slavery in Missouri, 1804-1865," pp. 63-64.)
8. In the 1530s, "an Arabian black" named Estéban, in company with Cabeza de Vaca and two other Spaniards, is believed to have traveled as far west as Arizona, at which time he may have seen the Pacific at the Gulf of California in northern Mexico. (Bernard DeVoto, *The Course of Empire*, pp. 17-21.)
9. Reuben G. Thwaites, ed., *Original Journals of the Lewis and Clark Expedition, 1804-1806*, 2:358.

Chapter 1

1. Writers about the expedition have universally maintained that Jefferson summoned Lewis from his military duties on the frontier to Washington in 1801 in order to prepare him for a transcontinental exploration. Donald Jackson, however, convincingly refutes this in an article revealing that Jefferson's initial use of Lewis was to have him assist in evaluating members of the army's officer corps. Jackson concludes that Jefferson probably did not decide to send out an expedition until "much later than has been previously believed." (Donald Jackson, "Jefferson, Meriwether Lewis, and the Reduction of the United States Army," p. 96.)
2. Milo M. Quaife, ed., *The Journals of Captain Meriwether Lewis and Sergeant John Ordway*, p. 31. When Lewis dated his departure from Pittsburgh as August 30, he was in error by one day. Not only is his journal entry for the second day of the journey dated September 1, but in subsequent letters to Jefferson and Clark he said he started down the Ohio on August 31.

3. The journals of the expedition which survive to this day were written by Lewis, Clark, Sergeant Charles Floyd, Sergeant John Ordway, Private Joseph Whitehouse, and Sergeant Patrick Gass, although Gass's survives only in paraphrased form, the original having been lost. Private Robert Frazer is known to have kept a journal, but it was never published and has disappeared. Because Lewis ordered all the sergeants to keep journals, it is assumed that Sergeant Nathaniel Pryor also kept one; however, none has ever come to light. (For a fascinating account of what happened to these journals over the years, see Paul R. Cutright, *A History of the Lewis and Clark Journals.*)

4. Although Lewis had promised Clark a captain's commission, at the last minute the War Department came through with only that of a second lieutenant. Both he and Lewis were disappointed, but they agreed to keep the matter a secret (to the men of the expedition Clark was always "Captain"), and in all regards they exercised equality of command. There can be no question that Clark was offended by the lieutenancy. Upon the expedition's return, he wrote the secretary of war a curt letter of resignation.

   Donald Jackson names the "nine young men from Kentucky" who were inducted at the Falls of the Ohio, pointing out that two of them may already have been with Lewis when he arrived. (Donald Jackson, ed., *Letters of the Lewis and Clark Expedition with Related Documents, 1783-1854*, 1:118, n. 1; 1:125-26, n. 1.)

5. Ernest S. Osgood, ed., *The Field Notes of Captain William Clark, 1803-1805*, p. 8.

6. Ibid., p. 30.

7. Ibid., p. 32.

8. Reuben G. Thwaites, ed., *Original Journals of the Lewis and Clark Expedition, 1804-1806*, 1:16-17. Osgood, *Field Notes*, p.41.

9. Thwaites, *Journals*, 1:40.

10. Ibid., 1:53.

11. Osgood, *Field Notes*, p. 60.

12. Ibid., p. 110. Floyd was the only man to lose his life during the entire course of the expedition.

13. Thwaites, *Journals*, 1:143. On this same date, Sergeant Gass, who replaced Floyd as a noncommissioned officer, reported: "This day we saw several gangs or herds of buffaloe on the sides of the hills: One of our hunters killed one, and Captain Clarke's black servant killed two." (Patrick Gass, *A Journal of the Voyages and Travels of a Corps of Discovery*, p. 43.)

14. Ivan E. McDougle, *Slavery in Kentucky, 1792-1865*, p. 33. Also, see Emil Oberholzer, "The Legal Aspects of Slavery in Missouri," p. 338.

15. Osgood, *Field Notes*, p. 114.

16. Thwaites, *Journals*, 1:123.

17. Osgood, *Field Notes*, p. 119.

18. Thwaites, *Journals*, 1:165.

19. Osgood, *Field Notes*, p. 158.

20. Ibid. Thwaites, *Journals*, 1:186. Quaife, *Journals of Lewis and Ordway*, p. 154.

21. Jackson, *Letters*, 2:537. Immediately after the reference to the Arikara and Sioux women, Biddle's notes of his interview with Clark cryptically state, "Anecdote of York man afraid of him." Unfortunately, Biddle does not relate the anecdote. (Ibid., 2:538.)

22. Ibid., 2:503. Also, Elliott Coues, ed., *History of the Expedition under the Command of Lewis and Clark*, 1:164. The Coues edition of the journals, published in 1893, is an extensively annotated reissue of Nicholas Biddle's narrative version of the journals, published in 1814.

23. Coues, *History*, 1:164. The source of the story about the two Arikara girls aboard the keelboat is unclear, for it does not appear in Biddle's notes of his interview with Clark in 1810. In all probability, it was told by Clark himself or by Private George Shannon, who after the expedition spent some time with Biddle in Philadelphia, elaborating on information contained in the journals.

24. Osgood, *Field Notes*, p. 19.

Chapter 2

1. Reuben G. Thwaites, ed., *Original Journals of the Lewis and Clark Expedition, 1804-1806*, 1:209. Shortly after the expedition had arrived, Clark wrote, "we made up the presents and entertained Several of the Curious Chiefs whome, wished to see the Boat which was verry curious to them viewing it as great medison (*whatever is mysterious or unintelligible is called great medicine*) as they also Viewed my black Servent."

2. Elliott Coues, ed., *History of the Expedition under the Command of Lewis and Clark*, 1:243. Biddle was told about Le Borgne's visit by Clark. According to Biddle's notes, "The negro pulled off the hand[kerchie]f from his head & shewed his hair—on which The Borgne was convinced that he was of a different species from the whites." (Donald Jackson, ed., *Letters of the Lewis and Clark Expedition with Related Documents, 1783-1854*, 2:539.)

3. John Bakeless, *Lewis & Clark*, p. 269.

4. Although Sacagawea has incorrectly been immortalized as the guide who pointed the way across the West, she did make at least six important contributions to the expedition's success. Her presence with her baby signaled that this was not a war party, accounting in part for the friendly reception the explorers received from most of the western tribes; she saved vital articles which washed overboard when the pirogue she was in almost capsized; she helpfully identified a few topographical features in her home country; her brother turned out to be the chief of the Shoshoni band Lewis and Clark met; her ability to speak Shoshoni not only aided the captains in their negotiations for horses, but also alerted them to the possibility that the band might leave to hunt buffalo before all the horses needed could be acquired; and her knowledge of how to procure and prepare edible plants was of great value in times when food was short.

5. Coues, *History*, 1:257.

6. Thwaites, *Journals*, 1:235.

7. Ibid., 1:243.

8. Ibid., 1:250.

9. Ernest S. Osgood, ed., *The Field Notes of Captain William Clark, 1803-1805*, p. 185.

10. Jackson, *Letters*, 1:315.

11. Thwaites, *Journals*, 1:284-85.

12. Jackson, *Letters*, 1:vii.

13. Milo M. Quaife, ed., *The Journals of Captain Meriwether Lewis and Sergeant John Ordway*, p. 209. Thwaites, *Journals*, 2:23.

14. Thwaites, *Journals*, 2:42.

15. Ibid., 2:25.

16. Ibid., 2:91.

17. Bernard DeVoto, ed., *The Journals of Lewis and Clark*, p. xlvi.

18. Thwaites, *Journals*, 2:122. Lewis took Sergeant Nathaniel Pryor, the interpreter George Drouillard, John Shields, Pierre Cruzatte, Jean Baptiste Lepage, and Richard Windsor. Clark's group consisted of Sergeant Patrick Gass, York, George Shannon, Joseph Field, and Reuben Field, the last two being brothers.

19. Ibid., 2:127.

20. Ibid., 2:181. The two captains differ as to where York was on the second day of the portage. Lewis says he remained at the lower camp below the falls, but Clark says the only ones left there were Sergeant Ordway, Silas Goodrich, Charbonneau, Sacagawea, and little "Pomp." Lewis was probably right, for Ordway wrote: "large gangs of buffalow all around the lower camp to day. one gang swam the river near the camp. Cap¹ Clarks Servant York killed one of them." Private Whitehouse's journal seems to confirm this. (Quaife, *Journals of Lewis and Ordway*, p. 235. Thwaites, *Journals*, 7:105.)

21. Thwaites, *Journals*, 2:188.

22. Ibid., 2:182-83.

23. Ibid., 2:199.

24. Ibid., 2:197.
25. Ibid.
26. Ibid., 2:199.
27. Ibid.
28. Ibid., 2:215.
29. Ibid., 2:214.
30. Ibid., 2:175.
31. Ibid.
32. Sergeant Gass's journal takes note of York on the day Clark's small advance party started out. The group evidently did some hunting for the men with the boats, for in the afternoon the main party came upon "a deer skin, that Captain Clarke's man had hung up." Private Whitehouse also mentions York's departure "to go up one or two days travel by land." (Patrick Gass, *A Journal of the Voyages and Travels of a Corps of Discovery*, p. 131. Thwaites, *Journals*, 7:116.)
33. Thwaites, *Journals*, 2:254.
34. Ibid., 2:262.
35. Ibid., 6:63.
36. Ibid. In the tables in Thwaites, the distance from "Yorks 8 Islands" to the Three Forks of the Missouri adds up to forty-six miles.
37. Ibid., 2:279.
38. Ibid., 2:339.
39. Ibid., 2:340.

Chapter 3

1. Reuben G. Thwaites, ed., *Original Journals of the Lewis and Clark Expedition, 1804-1806*, 2:350-51.
2. Ibid., 2:358.
3. Ibid., 2:356.
4. Ibid., 2:358. The man who told the Shoshonis about York must have been George Drouillard, the interpreter of sign language who was with Lewis at the time. In explaining how he was able to converse with Chief Cameahwait and the others, Lewis wrote, "The means I had of communicating with these people was by way of Drewyer [Drouillard] who understood perfectly the common language of jesticulation or signs which seems to be universally understood by all the Nations we have yet seen." (Ibid., 2:346.)
5. Elliott Coues, ed., *History of the Expedition under the Command of Lewis and Clark*, 2:506.
6. Thwaites, *Journals*, 2:363.
7. Patrick Gass, *A Journal of the Voyages and Travels of a Corps of Discovery*, p. 155.
8. Ella E. Clark, *Indian Legends from the Northern Rockies*, pp. 144-45. Also, see Olin D. Wheeler, *The Trail of Lewis and Clark, 1804-1904*, 2:65-66. Basing his account on a Flathead legend, John Bakeless writes: "York made his usual impression and had to submit to the inevitable test of his blackness with wet red forefingers. His strength likewise astonished the Flatheads, as did the fact that he could cook." This and several other references to York as a cook tend to support those who contend this was his role, but, as noted earlier, the journals are vague on the subject. Perhaps, as did others, he took his turn cooking from time to time in one or another of the messes into which the squads were broken down. (John Bakeless, *Lewis & Clark*, p. 261.)
9. Thwaites, *Journals*, 3:63, 66, 69. During the crossing, several colts were eaten and an experimental army ration in the form of "portable soupe" was consumed. (Ibid., 3:71.)
10. Ibid., 5:98.
11. Ibid., 3:89.

12. Kate C. McBeth, *The Nez Perces Since Lewis and Clark*, p. 21. Clark, *Indian Legends*, p. 71. Miss McBeth was a missionary who lived among the Nez Perces for more than twenty-seven years, joining them in 1879 and learning to speak their language fluently.

13. Bakeless, *Lewis & Clark*, p. 268.

14. Thwaites, *Journals*, 3:111.

15. Ibid., 3:143.

16. Ibid., 3:105.

17. J.T. Dizney to Eva Emery Dye, 21 December 1903, Oregon Historical Society.

18. Frank White to Eva Emery Dye, 2 February 1904, Oregon Historical Society.

19. Thwaites, *Journals*, 3:154.

20. Ibid., 3:161.

21. Bernard DeVoto, ed., *The Journals of Lewis and Clark*, p. xlvii.

22. Hubert H. Bancroft, *History of the Northwest Coast, 1543-1800*, p. 189.

23. Thwaites, *Journals*, 3:207, fn. 1.

24. Ibid., 3:213, 216.

25. Ibid., 3:228.

26. Although Sergeant Gass wrote that "the party were consulted by the Commanding Officers," the vote apparently was genuine, with Lewis and Clark abiding by it. In Clark's words, "the Solicitations of every individual, except one of our party induced us [to] Conclude to Cross the river and examine the opposit Side." (Gass, *Voyages and Travels*, pp. 204-5. Thwaites, *Journals*, 3:246-47, 249.)

   Sacagawea also had a voice in making the decision. While she was not listed in the table of the vote compiled by Clark, just below it he notes that she was "in favour of a place where there is plenty of Potaˢ," evidently meaning the wapato, a potato-like plant with edible roots. Whether or not she was the first woman to vote in the Oregon country, as Dr. Chuinard maintains, she definitely was permitted to express her opinion. (Thwaites, *Journals*, 3:247. Eldon G. Chuinard, M.D., *Only One Man Died*, p. 335, fn. 1.)

27. Thwaites, *Journals*, 3:270.

28. Ibid., 3:293. Clark's use of the word *boy* should not be taken to mean that York was a youth. Southerners commonly referred to male slaves as *boys* until they reached such a mature age they became *uncles*.

29. Ibid., 3:296.

30. Ibid., 3:302. The various journalists are often unintentionally and delightfully amusing because of their odd misspellings and ambiguous sentence structures. A good example of the latter is Sergeant Ordway's entry for 1 January 1806: "The party Saluted our officers at day break this morning by firing at their quarters as a rememberence of the new year." (Milo M. Quaife, ed., *The Journals of Captain Meriwether Lewis and Sergeant John Ordway*, p. 319.)

31. Thwaites, *Journals*, 3:302.

Chapter 4

1. Patrick Gass, *A Journal of the Voyages and Travels of a Corps of Discovery*, p. 237. Among other statistics Gass compiled is that only seven of the thirty-three members of the expedition did not use tobacco, that just before the return journey the supply of moccasins came to "338 pair," and that "131 elk and 20 deer" were killed between 1 December 1805 and 20 March 1806. (Ibid., pp. 226-27, 229.)

2. Reuben G. Thwaites, ed., *Original Journals of the Lewis and Clark Expedition, 1804-1806*, 3:315.

3. Ibid., 3:311.

4. The brig *Lydia* not only narrowly missed meeting the Lewis and Clark party in early November, but also the following spring when it returned from Nootka Sound. Of the second

visit, a crew member wrote, "We proceeded about ten miles up the river, to a small Indian village, where we heard from the inhabitants, that Captains Clark and Lewis, from the United States of America; had been there about a fortnight before, on their journey over-land, and had left several medals with them, which they showed us." (John R. Jewitt, *Narrative of the Adventures and Sufferings of John R. Jewitt*, p. 161.)

5. Thwaites, *Journals*, 6:209.
6. See pages 159, n. 3; 162, n. 3.
7. Elliott Coues, ed., *The Manuscript Journals of Alexander Henry*, 2:914. Thwaites, *Journals*, 4:180-81. Comowool either was given one of these papers or found the one Lewis and Clark had "paisted up in our room" at Fort Clatsop. In 1814, Comowool showed the paper to Alexander Henry of the Northwest Company, who copied it into his journal.
8. Thwaites, *Journals*, 4:304.
9. Ibid., 4:358. Two remarkable cures took place while the expedition was with the Nez Perces, but neither was due to Clark. John Shields recommended steam baths followed by immersion in cold water for William Bratton, who had long been unable to walk or sit upright without pain, and it worked. As a result, a Nez Perce chief who had been paralyzed for years was given a somewhat similar treatment and gradually recovered the use of his limbs.
10. Ibid., 5:38.
11. Ibid., 5:98.
12. Ibid., 5:140, 142.
13. Ibid., 3:58.
14. Ibid., 5:183.
15. Ibid., 5:223. The wounded Indian returned Lewis's fire, narrowly missing him. In Lewis's words, "being bearheaded I felt the wind of his bullet very distinctly." No statement in the journals says the Blackfoot shot by Lewis died, but in a later letter Lewis wrote that two had been killed. Whether this was an assumption or a fact is unclear. (Ibid., 5:225. Donald Jackson, ed., *Letters of the Lewis and Clark Expedition with Related Documents, 1783-1854*, 1:342.)
16. Thwaites, *Journals*, 5:278, 290; 6:224.
17. Ibid., 6:75. "Yorks dry river" appears in Clark's record of distances along the Missouri, printed by Thwaites in a separate volume. In the journals themselves, Clark described the tributary in these words: "its chanel is 88 yards and in this there is not more water than could pass through an inch auger hole. [*I call it Yorks dry R.*]." (Ibid., 5:309-10.)
18. Ibid., 5:319.
19. Colter did not return to the frontier until 1810. While in the West, he discovered—or is usu-ally credited with having discovered—the areas of Jackson Hole, Wyoming, and Yellowstone National Park. Charbonneau and Sacagawea later took "Pomp" to St. Louis and left him there in the care of Clark. When eighteen, he met Prince Paul Wilhelm of Württemberg, went to Europe with him, and is said to have become fluent in four lan-guages. Returning to the West, he adopted the life of a trapper and guide, associating with such famous figures as Kit Carson, Jim Bridger, and John C. Frémont. He died in Oregon in 1866. (See Irving W. Anderson, "A Charbonneau Family Portrait.")
20. Thwaites, *Journals*, 5:394.
21. Richard Edwards and M. Hopewell, *Edwards's Great West*, p. 292. Published in 1860, this book's description of the welcome given the explorers was evidently based on word-of-mouth accounts handed down in St. Louis from the time of Lewis and Clark.

Chapter 5

1. Bernard DeVoto, *The Course of Empire*, p. 618.
2. Elliott Coues, ed., *History of the Expedition under the Command of Lewis and Clark*, 1:159, fn. 31.

3. Ibid. When Coues later comes to Lewis's remark about York having seen a scarlet bird as large as a pheasant near Fort Clatsop (see p. 44), he writes, "No bird of any such description exists in North America." Then he refers the reader back to the above footnote in which he characterizes York as a man who "used to get drunk and tell funny stories." By doing so, Coues as much as says the sighting of the bird was a pure invention and therefore further support of his claim that York's "glib tongue" was not to be trusted. Although Coues was an eminent ornithologist and we must accept his view that the bird as described does not exist, he made no allowance for the possibility the description was garbled by either York or Lewis, and one can only wonder whether he would have been as harsh had the sighting been reported by another member of the expedition. (Ibid., 3:1293, fn. 4.)

4. Perhaps this statement should be amended slightly in light of the many critical words which have been written about Toussaint Charbonneau, who on the whole comes through the pages of the journals as a man of less than admirable traits. Unlike York, however, in recent years more sympathetic interpretations of him have been advanced.

5. Eva Emery Dye's correspondence is in the possession of the Oregon Historical Society and contains, among other interesting items, family recollections of what some former members of the expedition had said about their experiences. Because Mrs. Dye subtitled her novel *The True Story of Lewis and Clark*, and because she listed an impressive array of sources at the beginning of it, some writers have indiscriminately accepted her words as reliable history.

6. Eva Emery Dye, *The Conquest*, pp. 195, 209, 324.

7. During his interview in 1810 with Nicholas Biddle, Clark told him that when the expedition withdrew briefly from the Bitterroots at the start of the return journey and its scientific instruments were left unattended, there was no concern any passing Indian would touch them, "because they were conceived to be great medicine & therefore sacred." (Donald Jackson, ed., *Letters of the Lewis and Clark Expedition with Related Documents 1783-1854*, 2:544.)

8. Pierre Antoine Tabeau, *Tabeau's Narrative of Loisel's Expedition to the Upper Missouri*, p. 201.

9. Ella E. Clark, *Indian Legends from the Northern Rockies*, p. 70. Another Nez Perce legend says most of the tribe deliberated killing Lewis and Clark and their men, but were dissuaded by a Nez Perce woman variously called Watkuweis and Wat-ku-ese. Years before, she had been abducted by the Blackfeet and in time was bought and treated with kindness by whites, probably in Canada. After an epic journey, she eventually returned home, where she was dying when the expedition frightened the Nez Perces with its sudden appearance. She is supposed to have told her tribesmen, "These are the people who helped me! Do them no hurt!" (Lucullus V. McWhorter, *Hear Me, My Chiefs!* p. 17. Also, Kate C. Mc-Beth, *The Nez Perces Since Lewis and Clark*, pp. 24-26.)

10. Reuben G. Thwaites, ed., *Original Journals of the Lewis and Clark Expedition, 1804-1806*, 3:136-37.

11. Ibid., 2:358.

12. Ibid.

Chapter 6

1. Approximately thirty books having something to do with Lewis and Clark were published between 1902 and 1958, a period chosen because its end roughly corresponds with the time when the portrayal of blacks as comic stereotypes became publicly unacceptable. (As an example of the way things were changing, the Columbia Broadcasting System removed the "Amos 'n' Andy" television series burlesquing blacks from the network in 1953.) Even though the estimate of thirty books includes a number in which the expedition is a secondary theme or York is barely mentioned, the nine books depicting him unfavorably still account for almost one-third of all the books appearing about Lewis and Clark in the

first six decades of this century. Seven of the nine books are identified in the following notes 2 through 8. The other two are both novels: Eva Emery Dye's *The Conquest* and Hidegarde Hawthorne's *Westward the Course.*

2. To say that Charles M. Wilson's *Meriwether Lewis of Lewis and Clark* is irresponsible is an understatement. Although presented as a legitimate biography, it is nothing more than a preposterous amalgam of elementary factual errors, ridiculous assertions with no foundation whatever, and transparent lifts from works of fiction—all without benefit of a single footnote. In his review of it, Professor Allan Nevins wrote, with reference to whether Lewis killed himself or was murdered, "Perhaps it *was* suicide; perhaps Meriwether Lewis had a premonition of this biography." (Allan Nevins, "Rewriting History," p. 770.)

3. Emerson Hough, *The Magnificent Adventure*, pp. 139-40.

4. Donald Culross Peattie, *Forward the Nation*, p. 115. York was not the only one made to speak with an absurd dialect. In many of the novels quoted from in this chapter, particularly those written earlier in the century, Sergeant Patrick Gass is given a comic Irish brogue, "begorra" and all. This, too, was once a standard literary device, but it went out of favor long before the thoughtless mocking of blacks was seen to be offensive. There is no explaining why so many writers have assumed that Gass was Irish, except possibly for the name Patrick. Actually, he was born in Pennsylvania, and, according to a letter written by his daughter, his father had been born in Maryland and his mother was "Martha Jane McLane, a scotch Lady." (Mrs. George Brierley to Eva Emery Dye, 6 January 1902, Oregon Historical Society.)

5. Charles M. Wilson, *Meriwether Lewis of Lewis and Clark*, pp. 128, 253.

6. Ibid., p. 128.

7. Kelsie Osborne, *Peaceful Conquest*, p. 30. Essentially the same statement making York and Scannon the only two disciplined members of the party appears in Albert and Jane Salisbury, *Two Captains West*, p. 23.

8. Vardis Fisher, *Tale of Valor*, p. 219. Wilson, *Lewis of Lewis and Clark*, pp. 101-2. Fisher, *Tale of Valor*, p. 87. Ethel Hueston, *Star of the West*, p. 47.

9. John Bakeless, *Lewis & Clark*, p. 276.

10. Richard Dillon, *Meriwether Lewis*, p. 92.

11. Ernest S. Osgood, ed., *The Field Notes of Captain William Clark, 1803-1805*, p. 159, fn. 1.

12. Ibid., p. 158.

13. Reuben G. Thwaites, ed., *Original Journals of the Lewis and Clark Expedition, 1804-1806*, 1:186.

14. William Clark Kennerly, *Persimmon Hill*, p. 19.

15. Milo M. Quaife, ed., *The Journals of Captain Meriwether Lewis and Sergeant John Ordway*, p. 154.

16. Thwaites, *Journals*, 1:186.

17. Ibid., 1:185. Osgood, *Field Notes*, p. 158.

18. Kenneth M. Stampp, *The Peculiar Institution*, p. 145.

Chapter 7

1. Vardis Fisher, *Tale of Valor*, p. 87. Donald Culross Peattie, *Forward the Nation*, pp. 102-103. Kelsie R. Osborne, *Peaceful Conquest*, p. 46. Albert and Jane Salisbury, *Two Captains West*, p. 41. Ibid.

2. William H. Grier, M.D., and Price M. Cobbs, M.D., *Black Rage*, p. 87.

3. Fisher, *Tale of Valor*, p. 138.

4. Ibid., pp. 92, 158, 410. Despite the line Fisher has Reuben Field speak—"That's the nigger's last chance before the Blackfeet scalp him"—there is no evidence in any of the journals that York's companions resented whatever relations he may have had with the Indian women. Actually, the subject never comes up.

5. Fisher now and then somewhat moderates his negative portrayal of York by having his companions say such things as "he was all man, this big giant, for he never tried to shirk"

and "he did the work of two men." But the totality of the impression given is that York's excessive womanizing posed annoying problems for Lewis and Clark. (Ibid., p. 188.)

6. Olin D. Wheeler, *The Trail of Lewis and Clark, 1804-1904*, 1:135.

7. Elijah H. Criswell, *Lewis and Clark: Linguistic Pioneers*, p. xxxiv.

8. The captains name only a few men as having been treated for venereal disease, although by their own words it is evident that many more were infected. Before leaving the Mandan villages, Clark wrote that the disease had "been communicated to many of our party at this place," and at the Pacific Lewis blamed a group of Chinook women for having "communicated the venerial to so many of our party in November last." (Ernest S. Osgood, ed., *The Field Notes of Captain William Clark, 1803-1805*, p. 185. Reuben G. Thwaites, ed., *Original Journals of the Lewis and Clark Expedition, 1804-1806*, 4:170.)

9. Elliott Coues, ed., *History of the Expedition under the Command of Lewis and Clark*, 1:164.

10. Ibid.

11. Robert Penn Warren, *Brother to Dragons*, p. 178. Warren evidently was not very familiar with the expedition, for he makes York Lewis's, not Clark's, slave.

12. Calvin Tomkins, *The Lewis and Clark Trail*, p. 46.

13. John E. Rees, *Madame Charbonneau*, p. 23.

14. Ralph S. Space, *The Lolo Trail*, p. 29.

15. John Bakeless, *Lewis & Clark*, p. 268.

16. F.F. Gerard to Eva Emery Dye, 12 November 1889, Oregon Historical Society.

17. John F. McDermott, ed., *The Western Journals of Washington Irving*, p. 82.

18. There is, of course, no way of knowing whether this Nez Perce legend has an underlying stratum of substance to it, but, unlike many legends, it does not float in a vacuum without any support. Prior to Chief Joseph's War, William Henry Jackson, the noted pioneer photographer of the West, took a picture of a Nez Perce half-breed with light hair and blue eyes who, other Nez Perces told him, was the son of William Clark. (A copy of this photograph is in the Iconographic Collections of the Wisconsin Historical Society.) Also, after Chief Joseph surrendered, General Nelson Miles learned that one of his prisoners, presumably the same man, claimed to be the son of Clark. In addition, Nathaniel Langford, a prominent early Montana figure who knew the man Jackson photographed, wrote: "During my residence in Montana I often met this half blood son of Captain Clark. He was very proud of his paternal ancestry, and, when accosted, would straighten his body to its full height and strike his chest with his open palm, exclaiming as he did so: 'Me Clark!'" (Alvin M. Josephy, Jr., *The Nez Perce Indians and the Opening of the Northwest*, pp. 13-14, fn. 6. Lucullus V. McWhorter, *Hear Me, My Chiefs!* p. 498. For the Langford quote, an unsigned article with a photograph of the alleged son entitled "What Are the Facts? Did Capt. William Clark Leave Indian Decendents [sic]?" in *Montana, the Magazine of Western History*, p. 37.)

Chapter 8

1. Richard Edwards and M. Hopewell, M.D., *Edwards's Great West*, p. 292.

2. Elliott Coues, ed., *History of the Expedition under the Command of Lewis and Clark*, 1:159, fn. 31.

3. Donald Culross Peattie, *Forward the Nation*, p. 261.

4. Charles G. Clarke, *The Men of the Lewis and Clark Expedition*, p. 38.

5. Letters to writer from Frances H. Stadler, Archivist, Missouri Historical Society, 26 July 1979 and 17 October 1979. Despite a search by Mrs. Stadler for the documents Clarke ascribed to the Society and despite her written request of Clarke to identify the documents he referred to, none justifying his assertions was found.

6. John F. McDermott, ed., *The Western Journals of Washington Irving*, p. 82.

7. The first publication of Irving's notes was by the Bibliophile Society of Boston in 1919.

8. Edwards and Hopewell, *Edwards's Great West*, p. 292.

9. J. Thomas Scharf, *History of St. Louis City and County*, 1:311.

Chapter 9

1. K.D. Curtis, "York, the Slave Explorer," pp. 12-14.

2. Ibid., p. 11.

3. While Curtis says York "discovered new wildlife species" and Eva Emery Dye has him an amateur scientist making "some fabulous finds," neither gives the reader any inkling of what he is supposed to have discovered. The only two references in the journals to York and wildlife are when he told Lewis he had seen a large scarlet bird and when he showed Clark a tobacco worm. From this it would appear that the fabulous finds were made by Curtis and Dye about York, not by York himself. (Eva Emery Dye, *The Conquest*, p. 245.)

4. William L. Katz, *Eyewitness: The Negro in American History*, p. 68.

5. L.R. Masson, ed., *Les Bourgeois de la Compagnie du Nord-Ouest*, 1:336-37.

6. Among others who have perpetuated the myth that York could speak French was no less an authority on the American frontier than Frederic Paxon. In the students' edition of his history of the frontier, he wrote that "when Lewis wanted to converse with the Indians [who understood French, but not English], he was forced to rely upon his mulatto body servant, who by chance spoke French." By describing York as a mulatto, by explaining his ability to speak French on the grounds he had learned it "by chance," and by making him Lewis's, not Clark's, slave, Paxon revealed that he had not done his Lewis and Clark homework. Donald Jackson reports still another textbook—*Living in Our America*, by James I. Quillen and Edward Krug—in which it is stated "the only persons on the expedition who spoke French were Charbonneau the guide, and York the Negro slave." (Frederic L. Paxon, *History of the American Frontier, 1763-1893*, p. 136. Donald Jackson, "The Public Image of Lewis and Clark," p. 3.)

7. John Clark's will, 24 July 1799, and codicil, 26 July 1799, Archives and Records Service, Jefferson County, Kentucky. Pierre Antoine Tabeau, *Tabeau's Narrative of Loisel's Expedition to the Upper Missouri*, p. 201.

8. Donald Jackson, ed., *Letters of the Lewis and Clark Expedition with Related Documents, 1783-1854*, 1:367. Who was McKenzie's mulatto who spoke bad French and worse English? Only a guess can be made. A number of the members of the expedition spoke the less than pure French of the frontier, as well as less than good English, among them several born of white and Indian marriages. Perhaps one of them—even Labiche himself, who is reported to have been half Omaha—served as an interpreter in this instance and was of such a dark complexion that McKenzie took him to be a mulatto.

9. Phillip T. Drotning, *An American Traveler's Guide to Black History*, p. vi. From the preface by Senator Edward W. Brooke.

10. Ibid., p. 117.

11. Nicholas Polos, "Explorer with Lewis and Clark," p. 90.

12. Ibid.

13. Ibid. In his footnote incorrectly quoting Donald Jackson, Polos makes no sense at all. With two uses of "*sic*" he seemingly corrects Jackson as follows: "A Slave [*sic*] bequeathed to Clark by his father John Clarke [*sic*], in a will dated 24 July 1799." Actually, Jackson wrote no such thing, neither spelling the word *slave* with a capital *S* nor the name *Clark* with a terminal *e*. (See Jackson, *Letters*, 1:319, n. 1.)

Chapter 10

1. The experience of a Kentucky slave named William illustrates the importance attached to being a young master's playmate: "To be young master's play boy was a coveted honor, as William well knew, which would later enable him to become a house servant, one of the most desirable positions on the whole plantation." The quotation "little Negro boy, York" comes from William Clark Kennerly, whose reliability as a source will be discussed a little

farther on in the text. (J. Winston Coleman, Jr., *Slavery Times in Kentucky*, pp. 48-50. William Clark Kennerly, *Persimmon Hill*, p. 12.)

2. Frederick Douglass, *My Bondage and My Freedom*, p. 35.

3. John Clark's will, 24 July 1799, and codicil, 26 July 1799, Archives and Records Service, Jefferson County, Kentucky. Although the will mentions twenty slaves by name, it leaves out the names of others, referring to them only as "the children of said negroes." It is therefore not possible to determine how many slaves John Clark owned, but it was certainly no less than twenty-seven. Eight were left directly to William: the five named in the text and "three old Negroes," James, Cupid, and Harry. At least three others—Ben, Priscilla, and her "present increase"—were left to him indirectly in that when his two nephews, John and Benjamin O'Fallon, reached the age of twenty-one, these slaves would become his. William either had been given or had acquired on his own some slaves before his father's death, because only a month later a list of his property included twenty-one.

4. In his excellent book on Lewis and Clark, Roy Appleman writes, "About the same age as Clark or possibly younger, York, who was married to a girl named 'Rose,' had been his lifelong companion and had been bequeathed to him by his father." Responding to an inquiry as to how he had come to the conclusion Rose was York's wife, Appleman explained that in the will the words "Also old York" had been inserted with a caret mark as an afterthought. This would have made the sentence before it was amended read, "I also give unto my son William one Negroe man named York, and his Wife Rose, and their two Children Nancy and Juba." However, while it is true the words "Also old York" do appear as an insertion in a copy of the will in the Jefferson County Will Book, they are not an insertion in the original will itself, where the complete sentence reads, "I also give unto my son William one Negroe man named York, Also old York, and his Wife Rose, and their two Children Nancy and Juba." There can therefore be no question that "old York" and Rose were the married couple. Conclusive evidence that Rose was not York's wife can be found in an 1811 letter, to be quoted on p. 112. In it we are told York was married to an unnamed slave woman belonging to a family having no connection with the Clarks. (Roy E. Appleman, *Lewis and Clark*, p. 56. Letter to writer from Appleman, 3 March 1979. Confirming that the insertion appears only in a copy of the will is a letter to writer of 5 April 1979 from Dr. Samuel W. Thomas, Director, Archives and Records Service, Jefferson County, Kentucky.)

5. A parenthetical comment in the will states that Rose had two other children, "Scippio and Daphny (Roses Children)," who were bequeathed to William Clark's brother Edmund. Because the will is silent as to whether "old York" was their father, it is possible Rose had these children by another husband and married "old York" after York was born. However, there being no further information about this matter, it cannot be assumed that York's mother was someone other than Rose.

6. The information regarding the slave dance called the juba, the African origin of the personal name Juba, and the practices having to do with the naming of slaves was obtained from the Schomburg Center for Research in Black Culture, New York, N.Y.

7. Will Durant, *Ceasar and Christ*, p. 466. Also, J.W. Haywood, Jr., "Juba II—African King," pp. 166, 169.

8. Regarding the naming of slaves, John Blassingame writes: "Memories of Africa were important in the development of self-awareness in slave children. In the seventeenth and eighteenth centuries, the slaves drew on these memories for their naming practices. Consequently, until the nineteenth century, African cognomens were prominent in any list of slaves. From around 1750 to the 1830s masters steadily encroached on slave naming practices, and by the latter date the bondsmen's cognomens had been anglicized and they exercised less autonomy in this area." (John W. Blassingame, *The Slave Community.* pp. 181-82).

9. Newbell N. Puckett, "American Negro Names," p. 40.

10. Kennerly was born in 1824 and seems to have seen William Clark on many occasions until Clark's death in 1838. Kennerly never knew York. His only reference to York's absence from the Clark household while he was growing up is when he says he received fencing lessons from "Rooskoski, a Pole who filled the position of valet to General Clark after the death of his faithful York." (Kennerly, *Persimmon Hill*, p. 31.)

11. Kennerly, *Persimmon Hill*, pp. 11-12, 47. The action Kennerly calls "the Dunmore Wars" is usually referred to as Lord Dunmore's War. In 1774, as Governor of Virginia, Lord Dunmore sent 3,000 militiamen to subdue Shawnee Indians on the colony's western frontier.

12. John L. Loos, "A Biography of William Clark, 1770-1813," p. 1.

13. Eugene D. Genovese, *Roll, Jordan, Roll*, p. 562.

14. William Clark Adreon, "Wm. Clark of the Village of St. Louis, Missouri Territory," a transcript of the address, with pages unnumbered.

15. Kentucky, where the Clarks settled in 1785, had no laws prohibiting slave literacy, but "public sentiment operated strongly against it." As late as 1844, some Southern states imposed the death penalty on slaves convicted for the second time of attempting to learn to read and write. (Coleman, *Slavery Times in Kentucky*, p. 78. Herbert Aptheker, ed., *A Documentary History of the Negro People in the United States: From Colonial Times through the Civil War*, p. 242.)

16. Harrison A. Trexler, "Slavery in Missouri, 1804-1865," p. 83.

17. Douglass, *Bondage and Freedom*, p. 42. Also, Blassingame, *Slave Community*, pp. 184-85.

18. Genovese, *Roll, Jordan, Roll*, pp. 502-3.

19. Ibid., p. 503.

20. Douglass, *Bondage and Freedom*, p. 89. White preachers regularly reminded slaves that they were cursed with "the sin of Ham," but one slave woman recalled her father interpreting the Old Testament in an ingenious way. In his view, Adam had been so terrified by his original sin that he had turned *white*. (Genovese, *Roll, Jordan, Roll*, p. 246. For an illuminating discussion of the belief that God's curse on Noah's son Ham caused all of Ham's descendants to be black, see Winthrop D. Jordan, *White over Black*, pp. 17-19.)

21. William H. Grier, M.D., and Price M. Cobbs, M.D., *Black Rage*, p. 66.

22. Kenneth M. Stampp, *The Peculiar Institution*, p. 305. Working from census figures, as well as from other sources, Stampp concludes that "the occurrence of various mild and acute 'forms of neurosis almost certainly exceeded the rate in twentieth-century urban populations." When describing their slaves, owners frequently noted that they stuttered and stammered, were easily excited and frightened, and displayed other symptoms the owners were at a loss to explain except with the catchall term "mentally unsound."

23. Chase C. Mooney, *Slavery in Tennessee*, p. 90. Also, Genovese, *Roll, Jordan, Roll*, p. 348.

24. Of the relationships between black and white children of the same plantation, Blassingame writes: "Often assigned as playmates to their young masters, black children played in promiscuous equality with white children. Together they roamed the plantation or went hunting, fishing, berry picking, or raiding watermelon and potato patches. Indeed, at first, bondage weighed lightly on the shoulders of the black child. Lunsford Lane, in reflecting on his childhood on a North Carolina plantation, wrote: 'I knew no difference between myself and the white children, nor did they seem to know any in turn.' " (Blassingame, *Slave Community*, pp. 183-84.)

25. James A. James, *The Life of George Rogers Clark*, p. 260.

Chapter 11

1. Eugene D. Genovese, *Roll, Jordan, Roll*, pp. 502, 517. While there seems to have been no set age for a slave boy to begin to function as a body servant, Genovese points out that most

began to perform their duties when their young masters first went off to school. In the case of Clark, he appears not to have gone to school away from home, so it can only be speculated that York began his training as a body servant at about the age of twelve, when slave children were usually selected to be either field hands or domestics.

2. J. Winston Coleman, Jr., *Slavery Times in Kentucky*, p. 49.

3. Ibid., p. 50.

4. Genovese, *Roll, Jordan, Roll*, pp. 351-52.

5. Strength was often one of the considerations given to the selection of a body servant. A former slave boy, recalling the physical competition he had to win in order to be chosen as his young master's companion, said, "We were all ordered to run, jump, wrestle, turn somersets, walk on our hands, and go through the various gymnastic exercises that the imagination of our brain could invent, or the strength and activity of our limbs could endure." (Coleman, *Slavery Times in Kentucky*, p. 48.)

6. Genovese, *Roll, Jordan, Roll*, p. 439. A visitor to Kentucky and Tennessee reported that he had heard little "nigger gibberish," and added that "coloured men in America seem to speak better, or at least more agreeably to an English ear, than the whites." (Chase C. Mooney, *Slavery in Tennessee*, p. 96.)

7. Ludie J. Kinkead, "How the Parents of George Rogers Clark Came to Kentucky in 1784-85," p. 2.

8. Daniel Drake, M.D., *Pioneer Life in Kentucky, 1785-1800*, p. 27. James A. James, *The Life of George Rogers Clark*, p. 325.

9. Samuel W. Thomas and Eugene H. Conner, M.D., "George Rogers Clark (1752-1818): Natural Scientist and Historian," p. 221, n. 6.

10. The text's details of frontier life in Kentucky are drawn mainly from Daniel Drake's *Pioneer Life in Kentucky, 1785-1800*. Drake's family moved to Kentucky in 1788, when he was about three years old, and he grew up there while the Clarks were living at Mulberry Hill. Clark, in a letter to Nicholas Biddle, told him he returned to "a Farm in Kentucky" when he resigned from the army in 1796. (Donald Jackson, ed., *Letters of the Lewis and Clark Expedition with Related Documents, 1783-1854*, 2:572.)

11. Coleman, *Slavery Times in Kentucky*, p. 15.

12. William H. English, *Conquest of the Country Northwest of the River Ohio, 1778-1783, and Life of Gen. George Rogers Clark*, 1:45.

13. Ibid., 1:147.

14. Reuben G. Thwaites, "William Clark: Soldier, Explorer, Statesman," p. 6.

15. Jackson, *Letters*, 2:575.

16. Jerome O. Steffen, *William Clark: Jeffersonian Man on the Frontier*, p. 28.

17. William Clark Kennerly, *Persimmon Hill*, p. 14.

18. Jackson, *Letters*, 2:572. Clark's movements during these years are taken from John L. Loos, "A Biography of William Clark, 1770-1813," pp. 59-63.

19. Mary Kennerly Taylor to Eva Emery Dye, undated, Oregon Historical Society. Mrs. Taylor was in error in saying that Julia Hancock was a few months older than Harriet Kennerly. Harriet was born in 1788, and Julia not until 1791.

20. On 10 January 1799, six months before their father's death, George Rogers sold William five slaves, including a man named Lew and a woman named Venos. Despite the difference in spelling, there is no question these were the same Lue and Venice (later called Venus in family recollections) who were bequeathed to him in John Clark's will. How he could sell them to William before he had inherited them is as much a mystery as are a number of other exchanges of property made within the family at this time. (Bond and Power of Attorney Book 2, Archives and Records Service, Jefferson County, Kentucky.)

21. As early as 12 December 1802, George Rogers wrote that William "is now settled at Clarksville in the Indiana Territory." (Jackson, *Letters*, 1:7.)

22. Thomas and Conner, "George Rogers Clark: Natural Scientist and Historian," p. 211.

23. Kennerly, *Persimmon Hill*, p. 19. Venus was undoubtedly the Venos and Venice of note 20 above and a good example of the versatility with which the different Clarks could spell the same words in different ways. Cupid was bequeathed to William in 1799, but turns up here as one of George Rogers's servants. Although confusion surrounds the disposition of many of the Clark family's slaves, it appears that their legal ownership sometimes had little to do with whom they served.

24. Jackson, *Letters*, 1:110-11. As has been noted by a number of writers, the slowness and uncertainty of the mails in those days could have turned the Lewis and Clark Expedition into the Lewis and Hooke Expedition. Lewis's letter of June 19 did not reach Clark until July 17, by which time Lewis had traveled as far as Pittsburgh and met a Lieutenant Moses Hooke. On July 26, he wrote Jefferson, "Should I recieve no answer from Mr. Clark previous to my leaving this place, or he decline going with me, I would be much gratifyed with being authorized to take Lieut. Hooke with me." Clark's letter of acceptance was soon received, however, and young Moses Hooke was relegated to a back seat in history. (Ibid., 1:114.)

25. Ibid., 1:58. Olin D. Wheeler, *The Trail of Lewis and Clark, 1804-1904*, 1:122. Wheeler says Willard in later years "enjoyed telling how his fine physique enabled him to pass the inspection for enlistment in the expedition," whereas more than one hundred failed.

26. Clark's use of the word *fat* is particularly puzzling in view of the description of York given by Pierre Antoine Tabeau, the Missouri River trader who was with the Arikaras when the expedition arrived. Simply describing York as "a large, fine man, black as a bear," he made no mention of obesity. Unless the words *fine man* refer to York's appeal as a person, not his appearance, Tabeau had an entirely different perception of York's physique than did Clark.

27. Jackson, *Letters*, 2:503. Reuben G. Thwaites, ed., *Original Journals of the Lewis and Clark Expedition, 1804-1806*, 1:185, 243. York is described as a man of "very large size" in Nicholas Biddle's notes of his interview with Clark at Fincastle, Virginia, in 1810. While Biddle apparently never met York, he asked Clark a number of questions about him, so this description presumably comes from Clark. In his narrative version of the journals, Biddle referred to York as "a remarkably stout, strong negro." (Elliott Coues, ed., *History of the Expedition under the Command of Lewis and Clark*, 1:159.)

28. While it is possible Lewis and Clark took York along because they somehow knew in advance that the color of his skin would be valuable to them with Indians who had never seen a black man, it is unlikely. The journals give the impression that the Indians' surprise at seeing a black man was a surprise to Lewis and Clark themselves.

Chapter 12

1. In recalling her father's strong likes and dislikes, Sergeant Gass's daughter wrote: "he did not like colored people. he was riding along with a man once during the Civil War & they were discussing that matter. the driver said he thought the negro as good as any white man. Father said he preferred to walk rather than ride with a man that expressed himself that way." (Mrs. George Brierley to Eva Emery Dye, 6 January 1902, Oregon Historical Society.)

York seems to have made a lasting impression on Private Alexander Willard. When asked whether he had ever heard his father talk about Lewis and Clark, Willard's son replied: "He told of their hardships, of their being compelled to eat their dogs. He spoke of 'Loyd' [Sergeant Floyd] and the negro man 'Yorke.' He did not speak much of Lewis but he was a personal friend of Gov. Clark and lived by him for years after the expedition was over." (Mrs. Lewis A. Willard to Eva Emery Dye, 25 February 1903, Oregon Historical Society.)

2. Frederick Douglass, *My Bondage and My Freedom*, p. 219.

3. Lloyd A. Hunter, "Slavery in St. Louis, 1804-1860," p. 264. A constant reminder to all St. Louis slaves that they were "subject to the whims of man and market" was the auction block, ironically located next to where justice was dispensed—"at the east door of the courthouse." (Ibid., p. 260.)

4. Ibid., pp. 256-57.

5. Elliott Coues, ed., *History of the Expedition under the Command of Lewis and Clark*, 1:159, fn. 31.

6. Bond and Power of Attorney Book 2, Archives and Records Service, Jefferson County, Kentucky. Clark freed Ben on 10 December 1802, but unaccountably the next day executed an instrument of indenture stating that in return for one dollar Ben bound himself to Clark until the end of 1832. Clark agreed to provide Ben with "sufficient meat, drink, wearing apparel and lodging," and at the expiration of his indenture to give him "one half acre lot of land in the town of Clarksville in the Indiana Territory a plough an axe and a hoe."

7. As an example of how infrequently masters had freed slaves by approximately the time the expedition returned, Kentucky's population in 1810 included 80,561 slaves and only 1,713 free blacks, or just slightly over two percent of the total black population. (Ivan E. McDougle, *Slavery in Kentucky, 1792-1865*, p. 8.)

8. William Clark Kennerly, *Persimmon Hill*, pp. 19-20.

9. George R.C. Sullivan to John O'Fallon, 2 June 1808, Missouri Historical Society. The slave Molly was later remembered by the wife of Clark's oldest son as "'Granny Molly,' the beloved colored nurse of the family." Granny Molly told Mrs. Meriwether Lewis Clark that when Julia Clark was on her deathbed, she said, "Oh watch over my Boy, and keep him neat, he is so beautiful Granny." (Mrs. Meriwether Lewis Clark to Eva Emery Dye, 27 May 1901, Oregon Historical Society.)

10. Kennerly, *Persimmon Hill*, p. 25.

11. Donald Jackson, ed., *Letters of the Lewis and Clark Expedition with Related Documents, 1783-1854*, 2:463, n. 7.

12. Ibid., 2:462.

13. William Clark memorandum book, 1809, Joint Collection, University of Missouri Western Historical Manuscript Collection—Columbia and State Historical Society of Missouri Manuscripts.

14. John O'Fallon to William Clark, 13 May 1811, Missouri Historical Society. O'Fallon was the son of Frances Clark, William's youngest sister.

15. Commenting on the deep attachments masters and slaves often developed for each other, the author of a scholarly and unsentimental study of slavery has written: "A slave who lived close to a warm, generous, and affectionate master often could not help but reciprocate these feelings, for the barriers of bondage and caste could not prevent decent human beings from showing sympathy and compassion for one another—slave for master as well as master for slave. The domestic's proverbial love for the white family was by no means altogether a myth. But it should be remembered that a slave's love for the good white people he knew was not necessarily a love of servitude, that a slave could wish to be free without hating the man who kept him in chains." (Kenneth M. Stampp, *The Peculiar Institution*, p. 379.)

16. The Mr. Fitzhugh of O'Fallon's letter was almost certainly Dennis Fitzhugh, Frances Clark's third husband, her first two having died. When O'Fallon says that "agreable to request" Fitzhugh had hired York out again, this time to a Mr. Mitchell, one can only conclude that the request had come from Clark.

17. Stampp, *The Peculiar Institution*, p. 68.

18. After stopping in Louisville to visit family for a few days, the Clarks continued on to Shelbyville, Kentucky, where they saw a newspaper reporting that Lewis had killed himself. While the question of whether he committed suicide or was murdered is still debated, most of those who have studied the matter dispassionately think he took his own life, as

did both Clark and Jefferson when they heard the news. Distraught over differences with the federal government about some of the drafts he had drawn, and fearing himself to be on the brink of financial ruin, Lewis is known to have been in an agitated state and to have been drinking heavily shortly before he met his end while traveling to Washington over the Natchez Trace. Strong feelings have arisen between disputants of the issue of suicide or murder, but those who favor the suicide theory make a more rational and persuasive case. (See Dawson A. Phelps, "The Tragic Death of Meriwether Lewis." Also, Jackson, *Letters*, 2:574-75.)

19. Stampp, *The Peculiar Institution*, pp. 84, 185.

20. Jackson, *Letters*, 1:58. According to Nicholas Biddle's notes of his interview with Clark in 1810, one of the questions he asked was "Qu: York has wife." Because he did not record the answer, it is unclear whether the question referred to York's marital status in 1810 or was a euphemism for inquiring into his relations with Indian women during the expedition. Since most of Biddle's notes have to do with Indians, the latter is the more likely possibility. (Ibid., 2:500.)

21. John W. Blassingame, *The Slave Community*, pp. 165-67. Some slaves varied the custom of jumping over a broomstick by jumping over it backwards. A former slave woman recalled that the one who did this without touching the handle would "boss de house," whereas if both did it they would be a congenial couple. (Ibid.)

22. Stampp, *The Peculiar Institution*, p. 344.

23. In his book on Lewis and Clark, Roy Appleman writes, "After the expedition, Clark freed all his slaves, including York in 1811, though he was ever afterwards interested in his welfare." As will be seen, Clark did not free all his slaves, but the issue here is the source of Appleman's statement that York was freed in 1811. Responding to an inquiry, he replied that he seemed to recall obtaining the information from the prospectus for a book entitled *Who's Who in the Wild West*, to be published by Marquis Who's Who, Inc. As it turns out, the book was never published, although the words about York in the prospectus have been found. Printed as an extract from a page in the proposed book, they read: "Just what York did after the expedition returned to St. Louis is unclear. But there is some evidence that he was living in Kentucky with his family on May 14, 1811, when his term of servitude expired." Just as there can be little question the writer of these words was aware of O'Fallon's letter, there can be little question he either had not read it or had not read it carefully. Totally misinterpreting the expiration of York's term of hire to Mr. Young to mean York had been released from slavery, the prospectus misled Appleman into thinking Clark had freed York in 1811. Not only did O'Fallon make it clear that York was still a slave at the time he wrote, but he obviously did not have the vaguest idea of what was to become of him. (Roy E. Appleman, *Lewis and Clark*, p. 252. Letter to writer from Appleman, 3 March 1979. Letter and photocopy of prospectus page to writer from Oscar B. Treiman, Vice President, Marquis Who's Who, Inc., 19 March 1979.)

Chapter 13

1. John F. McDermott, ed., *The Western Journals of Washington Irving*, p. 82.

2. There is no way of knowing whether the Richmond Irving mentions was Richmond, Virginia, or Richmond, Kentucky. In his book, Charles Clarke states unequivocally that it was Richmond, Kentucky, and in a later letter explains, "I based that it was in Kentucky upon logic," adding that he felt the distance was too far from Nashville for it to have been Richmond, Virginia. The chances are good that Clarke's logic was right, but his statement is nevertheless a conjecture, not a fact. (Charles G. Clarke, *The Men of the Lewis and Clark Expedition*, p. 38. Letter to writer from Clarke, 14 September 1978.)

3. In his will, written in 1837, Clark referred to ten slaves by name and others as "children," making it clear that he had not freed all of his slaves. In addition, a Missouri newspaper's account of Clark's funeral procession described his riderless horse being led by a slave "whose humid eyes told how deeply he lamented the loss of his paternal and indulgent master." (William Clark's will, 14 April 1837, Missouri Historical Society. Jerome O. Steffen, *William Clark: Jeffersonian Man on the Frontier*, p. 155).

4. Ira Berlin, *Slaves without Masters*, p. 60.

5. Ulrich B. Phillips, quoted by Eugene D.Genovese, "The Slave States of North America," p. 258. Also, see Winthrop D. Jordan, *White over Black*, pp. 577-78.

6. William Clark Kennerly, *Persimmon Hill*, p. 31.

7. Berlin, *Slaves without Masters*, p. 356.

8. Ibid., p. xiii.

9. Ibid., p. 327.

10. Chase C. Mooney, *Slavery in Tennessee*, pp. 11; 205, n. 23.

11. Herbert Aptheker, ed., *A Documentary History of the Negro People in the United States: From Colonial Times through the Civil War*, pp. 78, 153.

12. Berlin, *Slaves without Masters*, p. 99.

13. Ibid., pp. 222-23.

14. The white encroachment on even those relatively few former slaves who had learned trades was taking place long before York was freed. By way of illustration: "In 1783, white carpenters and bricklayers in Charleston, complaining that aggressive black tradesmen undercut their wages and lowered their standard of living, demanded legislation to prohibit Negroes from working on their own account. Such legislation was not passed at this time, but workingmen in other cities soon echoed these complaints and helped push free Negroes into an ever-shrinking range of menial occupations." (Berlin, *Slaves without Masters*, pp. 60-61.)

15. Richard C. Wade, *Slavery in the Cities*, p. 274.

16. Many free blacks became "wage slaves" in that charges for their food and clothing often amounted to as much as they earned. Berlin writes: "Once expenses were deducted there was little left, and free Negro workers frequently found themselves in debt to their employers. Sometimes they were obliged to sign on for another term under the same hard conditions." (Berlin, *Slaves without Masters*, p. 223.)

17. Berlin, *Slaves without Masters*, p. 223.

18. As two editors of a volume on free blacks have pointed out, "All were in desperate circumstances, so desperate that many freedmen sought the protection of renewed servile relationships with former masters." (David W. Cohen and Jack P. Greene, eds., *Neither Slave nor Free*, p. 13.)

19. William H. Grier, M.D., and Price M. Cobbs, M.D., *Black Rage*, p. 60.

20. All inquiries to county courthouses and historical societies throughout the Upper South have turned up no record of either York's manumission or death. In Jefferson County, Kentucky, manumissions were entered in Bond and Power of Attorney Books, but all of these books, except for three covering the years 1783-1805, have been lost or destroyed. If York was freed in Louisville, the record of his manumission was probably in one of the books which have disappeared.

21. Donald Jackson, ed., *Letters of the Lewis and Clark Expedition with Related Documents, 1783-1854*, 2:638-39. Although Clark's list appears on the cover of the book and conceivably could have been written at another time, Jackson says internal evidence points to it having been compiled during the years 1825-1828.

22. Mary Kennerly Taylor to Eva Emery Dye, undated, Oregon Historical Society.

23. Kennerly, *Persimmon Hill*, p. 52.

24. Harrison A. Trexler, "Slavery in Missouri, 1804-1865," p. 209. The Code of 1804, which

remained in effect until Missouri became a state in 1821, specified that a slave to be freed be "'sound in mind and body,' not over forty years of age or under twenty-one if a male, or eighteen if a female."

25. Kenneth M. Stampp, *The Peculiar Institution*, p. 232. Because Kentucky slaves could be freed only by a last will and testament or "an instrument of writing," if Clark freed his former body servant in Kentucky and was present to sign the instrument of writing, York could not have been freed before 1812. Clark did not leave St. Louis from the summer of 1810 until he took his family east two years later to remove them from the frontier during the War of 1812. While it is not known whether he stopped in Louisville on his way east, he did lay over there in October of 1812 on his return journey. (William Littell, *The Statute Law of Kentucky*, 2:387.)

26. In 1884, in a footnote based on a Charlottesville, Virginia, newspaper story, Hubert Howe Bancroft wrote: "Clarke's [for many years the name was often mistakenly spelled with an *e*] negro servant, York, mysteriously becomes Lewis; Captain Tom Lewis he called himself, if we may believe the authorities, which say that he was found on the road, frozen to death, in Albemarle County, Virginia, within about a mile of his own home, in the latter part of December, 1878. He was nearly ninety years old." This turns out to have been a misunderstanding on the newspaper's part. A former slave of the Lewis family, Tom had accompanied Reuben Lewis, Meriwether's brother, to the Mandan villages some years after the expedition, and his account of his travels in the West led those who did not know better to think he had been with Lewis and Clark. The newspaper apparently picked this up and assumed that York had changed his name to Tom Lewis. As a member of the Lewis family later wrote, when explaining the errors in the newspaper story, "We were struck with its incorrectness, but never guessed it would pass into history as an obituary of Yorke [*sic*]." (Hubert H. Bancroft, *History of the Northwest Coast, 1800-1846*, p. 85, fn. 45. Mrs. S.T.L. Anderson to Eva Emery Dye, 20 January 1902, Oregon Historical Society.)

Chapter 14

1. John C. Ewers, ed., *Adventures of Zenas Leonard, Fur Trader*, pp. 51-52.

2. Ibid., p. 139.

3. Ibid., p. 138.

4. Ibid., p. 147. Leonard's reference to the whole Crow nation being present is evidently an overstatement, for he earlier described the tribe as divided into two parts which seldom traveled and hunted together. In his words, "The Crow Nation contains from seven to eight thousand souls, and are divided into two divisions of an equal number in each—there being too great a number to travel together, as they could not get game in many places to supply such a force." (Ibid., p. 139.)

5. Ibid., p. 148.

6. Ibid., p. 153.

7. Hiram M. Chittenden, *The American Fur Trade of the Far West*, 2:687-88. This landmark work on the fur trade was published in 1902, long before the letter referred to and shortly to be quoted in the text came to light.

8. Reuben G. Thwaites, *Original Journals of the Lewis and Clark Expedition, 1804-1806*, 1:185, fn. 1. Thwaites, who in the early 1900s cast his vote for York having been the man Leonard met, almost surely was unaware of Washington Irving's notes of his conversation with Clark, which were not published until 1919.

9. The sources of the information contained in this paragraph are principally Capt. Reuben Holmes, "The Five Scalps," pp. 5-54; Willis Blenkinsop, "Edward Rose," in *The Mountain Men and the Fur Trade of the Far West*, 9:335-45; and Chittenden, *American Fur Trade*, 2:684-87.

10. Chittenden says Rose left the Crows not later than 1820 to reside with the Arikaras for the

next three years. There seems to be little doubt that he visited the Crows only twice in the 1820s: when he and Jedediah Smith wintered with them in 1823-1824, and when he briefly served as an interpreter for a treaty-making expedition in 1825. Although Chittenden states that after 1825 Rose "is mentioned now and then in connections that show him still among the Crows," he places him with the tribe in 1834, the year of the battle with the Blackfeet, solely on the basis of Leonard's narrative. (Dale L. Morgan, *Jedediah Smith and the Opening of the West*, pp. 88-89. Chittenden, *American Fur Trade*, 2:686-87.)

11. Burton Harris, *John Colter*, p. 59. The references to Rose having known Toussaint Charbonneau and Reuben Lewis are taken from Holmes, "The Five Scalps," pp. 19-22, 26.

12. National Archives, "Letters Received by the Office of Indian Affairs, 1824-80," St. Louis Superintendency, 1832-35, 10-46-5/M234, Roll 750. As best can be determined, the first mention of the existence of Sanford's letter was made by Stella M. Drumm, editor of "The Five Scalps," in 1938.

13. Beckwourth told his earliest biographer that he was with the Crows who pursued the Arikaras, at which time he said he identified the body of Rose. Gardner met Prince Maximilian when the latter visited the Upper Missouri in 1833-1834. (Delmont R. Oswald, ed., *The Life and Adventures of James P. Beckwourth, as Told to Thomas D. Bonner*, pp. 258-59. Maximilian, Prince of Wied, "Travels in the Interior of North America," in *Early Western Travels, 1748-1846*, 24:102-4.)

14. The author of a biographical sketch of Rose illustrates how this issue has not been faced head-on. He first says Leonard saw Rose lead the Crows in battle in 1834, then cites Sanford's letter reporting Rose to have been killed earlier. His only explanation for this obvious inconsistency is to say that Leonard "may have been incorrect in his date." (Blenkinsop, "Edward Rose," 9:345.)

15. Ewers, *Zenas Leonard*, p. xx.

16. Oswald, *Life and Adventures of Beckwourth*, p. xi. The information about Beckwourth in this paragraph can be found in Elinor Wilson, *Jim Beckwourth*, pp. 13-14, 30, 47-48, 78; Delmont R. Oswald, "James P. Beckwourth," in *The Mountain Men and the Fur Trade of the Far West*, 6:37-60; and throughout Oswald, *Life and Adventures of Beckwourth*.

17. In Leonard's narrative, "Mr. Mackinney" turns out to have been the renowned fur trader Kenneth McKenzie, who arrived in St. Louis and entered the fur trade in 1822. Although Beckwourth worked for him at a later date, he never traveled with him in the 1820s. Beckwourth's only trips up the Missouri in the 1820s were with William H. Ashley in 1824 and with Jedediah Smith in 1825. (Ray H. Mattison, "Kenneth McKenzie," in *The Mountain Men and the Fur Trade of the Far West*, 2:217-24.)

18. Wilson, *Jim Beckwourth*, p. 18.

19. Charles Kelly and Dale L. Morgan, *Old Greenwood*, p. 87. It should be noted that there was no love lost between Meldrum and Beckwourth, and it has been said that Meldrum may have forced Beckwourth to leave the Crows. (John E. Wickman, "Robert Meldrum," in *The Mountain Men and the Fur Trade of the Far West*, 9:281, fn. 8.)

20. The discrepancies between Beckwourth's description of the battle and Leonard's can be found by comparing Oswald, *Life and Adventures of Beckwourth*, pp. 189-95, with Ewers, *Zenas Leonard*, pp. 144, 155.

21. The number of black or mulatto trappers living with the Crows at this time is unrecorded. Beckwourth mentioned a mulatto who had taken the name of High Lance and there may have been others.

Chapter 15

1. It is no exaggeration to say that more is now known about York than is known about most of his fellow members of the expedition. With a few exceptions, they came from out of obscurity to join it and returned to obscurity when they were mustered out.

2. As a matter of passing interest, York's market value as a human being was not more than twenty-five times the $20 Lewis paid for Scannon, the Newfoundland dog. With reference to slave prices before 1830, "A prime male servant from eighteen to thirty-five years of age was in this early period worth from $450 to $500, and a woman about a fourth less." (Harrison A. Trexler, "Slavery in Missouri, 1804-1865," p. 38.)

3. Donald Jackson, ed., *Letters of the Lewis and Clark Expedition with Related Documents, 1783-1854*, 1:369.

4. Lewis also did not give any credit to Sacagawea in his letter to Henry Dearborn, although her husband, whom he characterized as "A man of no peculiar merit," received full compensation. Even Private John Newman, who had been discharged from the permanent party and sent back from the Mandan villages because of "mutinous expressions," was not overlooked. In view of his subsequent efforts to redeem himself, Lewis requested that he be given partial compensation. (Jackson, *Letters*, 1:365-66, 369.)

Bibliography

Unpublished Sources

Jefferson County Archives and Records Service, Louisville, Kentucky.
  Bill of sale of slaves from George Rogers Clark to William Clark, 10 January 1799.
  John Clark's will, 24 July 1799, and codicil, 26 July 1799.
  Instrument of manumission for William Clark's slave Ben, 10 December 1802.
  Instrument of indenture of Ben to William Clark, 11 December 1802.

Joint Collection, University of Missouri Western Historical Manuscript Collection—
Columbia and State Historical Society of Missouri Manuscripts, Columbia, Missouri.
  William Clark's memorandum book kept from 21 September 1809 until
  18 December 1809.

Missouri Historical Society, St. Louis, Missouri.
  George R.C. Sullivan to John O'Fallon, 2 June 1808.
  John O'Fallon to William Clark, 13 May 1811.
  William Clark's will, 14 April 1837.

National Archives, Washington, D.C.
  John F. A. Sanford to William Clark, 26 July 1833.

Oregon Historical Society, Portland, Oregon.
  F. F. Gerard to Eva Emery Dye, 12 November 1899.
  Mrs. Meriwether Lewis Clark to Eva Emery Dye, 27 May 1901.
  Mrs. George Brierley to Eva Emery Dye, 6 January 1902.
  Mrs. S. T. L. Anderson to Eva Emery Dye, 20 January 1902.
  Mrs. Lewis A. Willard to Eva Emery Dye, 25 February 1903.
  J. T. Dizney to Eva Emery Dye, 21 December 1903.
  Frank White to Eva Emery Dye, 2 February 1904.
  Mary Kennerly Taylor to Eva Emery Dye, undated.

Schomburg Center for Research in Black Culture, New York, New York.
  Information about the slave dance called the juba, the African origin of the personal
  name Juba, and the practices having to do with the naming of slaves.

Published Sources

Adreon, William Clark. "Wm. Clark of the Village of St. Louis, Missouri Territory." Paper
  presented to St. Louis Westerners, 16 January 1970.
Allen, John Logan. *Passage through the Garden: Lewis and Clark and the Image of the American North-
  west*. Urbana: University of Illinois Press, 1975.
Anderson, Irving W. "Sacajawea, Sacagawea, Sakakawea?" *South Dakota History* 8 (1978):
  303-11.
———. "A Charbonneau Family Portrait." *American West* 17 (1980): 4-13, 58-64.
Appleman, Roy E. *Lewis and Clark: Historic Places Associated with Their Transcontinental Explora-
  tion*. Washington: National Park Service, 1975.
Aptheker, Herbert, ed. *A Documentary History of the Negro People in the United States: From Colonial
  Times through the Civil War*. 1951. Reprint. Secaucus, N.J.: Citadel Press, 1973.

BIBLIOGRAPHY

Bakeless, John. *Lewis & Clark: Partners in Discovery.* New York: William Morrow & Co., 1974.

Bancroft, Hubert Howe. *History of the Northwest Coast, 1543-1800.* (*The Works of Hubert Howe Bancroft*, vol, 27.) San Francisco, A.L. Bancroft and Co., 1884.

_____. *History of the Northwest Coast, 1800-1846.* (*The Works of Hubert Howe Bancroft*, vol. 28.) San Francisco: A.L. Bancroft and Co., 1884.

Berlin, Ira. *Slaves without Masters: The Free Negro in the Antebellum South.* New York: Random House, Vintage Books, 1976.

Blassingame, John W. *The Slave Community: Plantation Life in the Antebellum South.* 2nd ed., revised and enlarged. New York: Oxford University Press, 1979.

Blenkinsop, Willis. "Edward Rose." In *The Mountain Men and the Fur Trade of the Far West*, 10 vols., edited by LeRoy R. Hafen, 9:335-45. Glendale: Arthur H. Clark Co., 1965-1972.

Chittenden, Hiram Martin. *The American Fur Trade of the Far West.* 1902. Reprint, 2 vols. Stanford: Academic Reprints, 1954.

Chuinard, Eldon G., M.D. *Only One Man Died: The Medical Aspects of the Lewis and Clark Expedition.* Glendale: Arthur H. Clark Co., 1979.

Clark, Ella E. *Indian Legends from the Northern Rockies.* Norman: University of Oklahoma Press, 1966.

Clark, William. "William Clark's Journal of General Wayne's Campaign." *Mississippi Valley Historical Review* 1 (1914): 418-44.

Clarke, Charles G. *The Men of the Lewis and Clark Expedition: A Biographical Roster of the Fifty-One Members and a Composite Diary of Their Activities from All Known Sources.* Glendale: Arthur H. Clark Co., 1970.

Cohen, David W., and Greene, Jack P., eds. *Neither Slave nor Free: The Freedman of African Descent in the Slave Societies of the New World.* Baltimore: The Johns Hopkins University Press, 1972.

Coleman, J. Winston, Jr. *Slavery Times in Kentucky.* Chapel Hill: University of North Carolina Press, 1940.

Coues, Elliott, ed. *History of the Expedition under the Command of Lewis and Clark.* 1893. Reprint, 3 vols. New York: Dover Publications, 1965.

_____, ed. *The Manuscript Journals of Alexander Henry, Fur Trader of the Northwest Company, and of David Thompson, Official Geographer and Explorer of the Same Company.* 1897. Reprint, 2 vols. Minneapolis: Ross & Haines, 1965.

Criswell, Elijah Harry. *Lewis and Clark: Linguistic Pioneers.* University of Missouri Studies, vol. 15, no. 2. Columbia: University of Missouri, 1940.

Curtis, K.D. "York, the Slave Explorer." *Negro Digest* (May 1962): 10-15.

Cutright, Paul Russell. *Lewis and Clark: Pioneering Naturalists.* Urbana: University of Illinois Press, 1969.

_____. *A History of the Lewis and Clark Journals.* Norman: University of Oklahoma Press, 1976.

Davis, David Brion. *The Problem of Slavery in the Age of Revolution, 1770-1823.* Ithaca: Cornell University Press, 1975.

Day, Judy, and Kedro, M. James. "Free Blacks in St. Louis: Antebellum Conditions, Emancipation, and the Postwar Era." *Bulletin* of the Missouri Historical Society 30 (1974): 117-35.

DeVoto, Bernard. *The Course of Empire.* Boston: Houghton Mifflin Co., 1952.

_____, ed. *The Journals of Lewis and Clark.* Boston: Houghton Mifflin Co., 1953.

Dillon, Richard. *Meriwether Lewis: A Biography.* New York: Coward-McCann, 1965.

Douglass, Frederick. *My Bondage and My Freedom.* 1855. Reprint. New York: Dover Publications, 1969.

Drake, Daniel, M.D. *Pioneer Life in Kentucky, 1785-1800.* Edited by Emmet Field Horine, M.D. New York: Henry Schuman, 1948.

Drotning, Phillip T. *An American Traveler's Guide to Black History.* Garden City: Doubleday & Co., 1968.

Durant, Will. *Caesar and Christ: A History of Roman Civilization and of Christianity from Their Beginnings to A.D. 325.* New York: Simon and Schuster, 1944.

Dye, Eva Emery. *The Conquest: The True Story of Lewis and Clark.* Chicago: A.C. McClurg & Co., 1902.

Edwards, Richard, and Hopewell, M., M.D. *Edwards's Great West.* St. Louis: Published at the offices of *Edwards's Monthly,* 1860.

Elkins, Stanley M. *Slavery: A Problem in American Institutional and Intellectual Life.* 3d ed., rev. Chicago: University of Chicago Press, 1976.

English, William Hayden. *Conquest of the Country Northwest of the River Ohio, 1778-1783, and Life of Gen. George Rogers Clark.* 2 vols. Indianapolis and Kansas City: Bowen-Merrill Co., 1896.

Ewers, John C., ed. *Adventures of Zenas Leonard, Fur Trader.* Norman: University of Oklahoma Press, 1959.

Filson, John. *The Discovery, Settlement and Present State of Kentucke.* 1784. Reprint. Gloucester, Mass: Peter Smith, 1975.

Fisher, Vardis. *Tale of Valor: A Novel of the Lewis and Clark Expedition.* Garden City: Doubleday & Co., 1958.

_____. *Suicide or Murder? The Strange Death of Governor Meriwether Lewis.* Denver: Alan Swallow, 1962.

Gass, Patrick. *A Journal of the Voyages and Travels of a Corps of Discovery, under the Command of Capt. Lewis and Capt. Clarke of the Army of the United States, from the Mouth of the River Missouri through the Interior Parts of North America to the Pacific Ocean, during the Years 1804, 1805 & 1806.* 1807. Reprint. Minneapolis: Ross & Haines, 1958.

Genovese, Eugene D. "The Slave States of North America." In *Neither Slave nor Free: The Freedman of African Descent in the Slave Societies of the New World,* edited by David W. Cohen and Jack P. Greene, pp. 258-77. Baltimore: The Johns Hopkins University Press, 1972.

_____. *Roll, Jordan, Roll: The World the Slaves Made.* New York: Random House, Vintage Books, 1976.

Greene, Lorenzo J.; Kremer, Garry R.; and Holland, Anthony F. *Missouri's Black Heritage.* St. Louis: Forum Press, 1980.

Grier, William H., M.D., and Cobbs, Price M., M.D. *Black Rage.* New York: Basic Books, 1968.

Haines, Aubrey L. "Johnson Gardner." In *The Mountain Men and the Fur Trade of the Far West,* 10 vols., edited by LeRoy R. Hafen, 2:157-59. Glendale: Arthur H. Clark Co., 1965-1972.

Harris, Burton. *John Colter: His Years in the Rockies.* New York: Charles Scribner's Sons, 1952.

Hawthorne, Hildegarde. *Westward the Course: A Story of the Lewis and Clark Expedition.* New York: Longmans, Green and Co., 1946.

Haywood, J.W., Jr. "Juba II—African King." *Negro History Bulletin* (May 1952): 166-69.

Hodge, Frederick Webb, ed. *Handbook of American Indians North of Mexico.* 2 vols. *Bulletin* of the Bureau of American Ethnology, 30. Washington: Government Printing Office, 1907.

Holmes, Reuben, Capt. "The Five Scalps." *Glimpses of the Past,* Missouri Historical Society, edited by Stella M. Drumm, 5 (1938): 3-54.

Hough, Emerson. *The Magnificent Adventure: This Being the Story of the World's Greatest Exploration, and the Romance of a Very Gallant Gentleman.* New York: D. Appleton and Co., 1923.

Howard, Harold P. *Sacajawea.* Norman: University of Oklahoma Press, 1971.

Hueston, Ethel. *Star of the West: A Romance of the Lewis and Clark Expedition.* New York and Chicago: A.L. Burt Co., 1935.

Hunter, Lloyd A. "Slavery in St. Louis, 1804-1860." *Bulletin* of the Missouri Historical Society 30 (1974): 233-65.

Jackson, Donald. "The Public Image of Lewis and Clark." *Pacific Northwest Quarterly* 57 (1966): 1-7.

_____. "A Footnote to the Lewis and Clark Expedition." *Manuscripts* 24 (1972): 3-21.

BIBLIOGRAPHY

———, ed. *Letters of the Lewis and Clark Expedition with Related Documents, 1783-1854.* 2d ed., with additional documents and notes. 2 vols. Urbana: University of Illinois Press, 1978.

———. "Jefferson, Meriwether Lewis, and the Reduction of the United States Army." *Proceedings* of the American Philosophical Society 124 (1980): 91-96.

———. *Thomas Jefferson & the Stony Mountains: Exploring the West from Monticello.* Urbana: University of Illinois Press, 1981.

Jacob, J.G. *The Life and Times of Patrick Gass, Now Sole Survivor of the Overland Expedition to the Pacific, under Lewis and Clark, in 1804-5-6.* Wellsburg, Va. (now W. Va.): Jacob & Smith, 1859.

James, James Alton. *The Life of George Rogers Clark.* Chicago: University of Chicago Press, 1928.

Jewitt, John R. *Narrative of the Adventures and Sufferings of John R. Jewitt, Only Survivor of the Crew of the Ship Boston, during a Captivity of Nearly Three Years among the Savages of Nootka Sound.* 1815. Reprint. Fairfield, Wash.: Ye Galleon Press, 1967.

Jordan, Winthrop D. *White over Black: American Attitudes toward the Negro, 1550-1812.* 1968. Reprint. New York: W.W. Norton & Co., 1977.

Josephy, Alvin M., Jr. *The Nez Perce Indians and the Opening of the Northwest.* abr. ed. New Haven: Yale University Press, 1971.

Katz, William Loren. *Eyewitness: The Negro in American History.* New York: Pitman Publishing, 1967.

Kelly, Charles, and Morgan, Dale L. *Old Greenwood: The Story of Caleb Greenwood, Trapper, Pathfinder, and Early Pioneer.* Georgetown, Calif.: Talisman Press, 1965.

Kennerly, William Clark. *Persimmon Hill: A Narrative of Old St. Louis and the Far West.* As told to Elizabeth Russell. Norman: University of Oklahoma Press, 1948.

Kinkead, Ludie J. "How the Parents of George Rogers Clark Came to Kentucky in 1784-1785." *History Quarterly* of the Filson Club 3 (1928): 1-4.

Littell, William. *The Statute Law of Kentucky, with Notes, Praelections, and Observations on the Public Acts.* 3 vols. Frankfort: Johnston & Pleasants, 1810.

Loos, John Louis. "A Biography of William Clark, 1770-1813." Ph.D. dissertation, Washington University, 1953.

McBeth, Kate C. *The Nez Perces Since Lewis and Clark.* New York: Fleming H. Revell Co., 1908.

McDermott, John Francis, ed. *The Western Journals of Washington Irving.* Norman: University of Oklahoma Press, 1944.

McDougle, Ivan E. *Slavery in Kentucky, 1792-1865.* 1918. Reprint. Westport, Conn.: Negro Universities Press, 1970.

McWhorter, Lucullus V. *Hear Me, My Chiefs! Nez Perce History and Legend.* Caldwell, Idaho: Caxton Printers, 1952.

Masson, L.R., ed. *Les Bourgeois de la Compagnie du Nord-Ouest.* 1889-1890. Reprint, 2 vols. New York: Antiquarian Press, 1960.

Mattison, Ray H. "Kenneth McKenzie." In *The Mountain Men and the Fur Trade of the Far West,* 10 vols., edited by LeRoy R. Hafen, 2:217-24. Glendale: Arthur H. Clark Co., 1965-1972.

Maximilian, Prince of Wied. "Travels in the Interior of North America." In *Early Western Travels, 1748-1846,* 32 vols., edited by Reuben Gold Thwaites, 22:25-24:346. Cleveland: Arthur H. Clark Co., 1904-1907.

Mooney, Chase C. *Slavery in Tennessee.* 1957. Reprint. Westport, Conn.: Negro Universities Press, 1971.

Morgan, Dale L. *Jedediah Smith and the Opening of the West.* Indianapolis: Bobbs-Merrill Co., 1953.

Nevins, Allan. "Rewriting History." *Saturday Review of Literature* 10 (June 1934): 770.

Oberholzer, Emil. "The Legal Aspects of Slavery in Missouri." *Bulletin* of the Missouri Historical Society 6 (1950): 333-51.

Osborne, Kelsie Ramey. *Peaceful Conquest: Story of the Lewis and Clark Expedition*. Portland: Lewis and Clark Sesquicentennial Committee for Oregon and Old Oregon Trail, Inc., 1955.

Osgood, Ernest Staples, ed. *The Field Notes of Captain William Clark, 1803-1805*. New Haven: Yale University Press, 1964.

Oswald, Delmont R. "James P. Beckwourth." In *The Mountain Men and the Fur Trade of the Far West*, 10 vols., edited by LeRoy Hafen, 6:37-60. Glendale: Arthur H. Clark Co., 1965-1972.

——, ed. *The Life and Adventures of James P. Beckwourth, as Told to Thomas D. Bonner*. 1856. Reprint. Lincoln: University of Nebraska Press, 1972.

Paxon, Frederic L. *History of the American Frontier, 1763-1893*. Students' ed. Boston: Houghton Mifflin Co., 1924.

Peattie, Donald Culross. *Forward the Nation*. New York: G.P. Putnam's Sons, 1942.

Phelps, Dawson A. "The Tragic Death of Meriwether Lewis." *William and Mary Quarterly* 13 (July 1956): 305-18.

Polos, Nicholas C. "Explorer with Lewis and Clark." *Negro History Bulletin* 45 (Oct., Nov., Dec. 1982): 90, 96.

Puckett, Newbell N. "American Negro Names." *Journal of Negro History* 23 (1938): 35-48.

Quaife, Milo Milton, ed. *The Journals of Captain Meriwether Lewis and Sergeant John Ordway*. Madison: State Historical Society of Wisconsin, 1916.

Rees, John E. *Madame Charbonneau: The Indian Woman Who Accompanied the Lewis and Clark Expedition*. Salmon, Idaho: Lemhi County Historical Society, 1970.

Reichard, Maximilian. "Black and White on the Urban Frontier: The St. Louis Community in Transition, 1800-1830." *Bulletin* of the Missouri Historical Society 33 (1976): 3-17.

Salisbury, Albert and Jane. *Two Captains West: An Historical Tour of the Lewis and Clark Trail*. Seattle: Superior Publishing Co., 1950.

Scharf, J. Thomas. *History of St. Louis City and County, from the Earliest Periods to the Present Day*. 2 vols. Philadelphia: Louis H. Everts & Co., 1883.

Skarsten, M.O. *George Drouillard: Hunter and Interpreter for Lewis and Clark and Fur Trader, 1807-1810*. Glendale: Arthur H. Clark Co., 1964.

Space, Ralph S. *The Lolo Trail: A History of Events Connected with the Lolo Trail Since Lewis and Clark*. Lewiston, Idaho: Printcraft Printing, 1970.

Sprague, Marshall. *So Vast So Beautiful a Land: Louisiana and the Purchase*. Boston: Little, Brown and Co., 1974.

Stampp, Kenneth M. *The Peculiar Institution: Slavery in the Ante-Bellum South*. New York: Alfred A. Knopf, 1978.

Steffen, Jerome O. *William Clark: Jeffersonian Man on the Frontier*. Norman: University of Oklahoma Press, 1977.

Strickland, Arvarh. "Aspects of Slavery in Missouri, 1821." *Missouri Historical Review* 65 (1971): 505-26.

Tabeau, Pierre Antoine. *Tabeau's Narrative of Loisel's Expedition to the Upper Missouri*. Edited by Annie Heloise Abel. Translated by Rose Abel Wright. Norman: University of Oklahoma Press, 1939.

Thomas, Samuel W. "William Clark's 1795 and 1797 Journals and Their Significance." *Bulletin* of the Missouri Historical Society 25 (1969): 277-95.

——, and Conner, Eugene H., M.D. "George Rogers Clark (1752-1818): Natural Scientist and Historian." *History Quarterly* of the Filson Club 41 (1967): 202-26.

Thwaites, Reuben Gold, ed. *Original Journals of the Lewis and Clark Expedition, 1804-1806*. 8 vols. New York: Dodd, Mead & Co., 1904-1905.

——. "William Clark: Soldier, Explorer, Statesman." *Collections* of the Missouri Historical Society 2 (1906): 1-24.

Tomkins, Calvin. *The Lewis and Clark Trail*. New York: Harper & Row, 1965.

BIBLIOGRAPHY

Trexler, Harrison Anthony. "Slavery in Missouri, 1804-1865." Ph.D. dissertation, The Johns Hopkins University, 1914.

Wade, Richard C. *Slavery in the Cities: The South, 1820-1860.* 1964. Reprint. New York: Oxford University Press, 1977.

Warren, Robert Penn. *Brother to Dragons: A Tale in Verse and Voices.* New York: Random House, 1953.

"What Are the Facts? Did Capt. William Clark Leave Indian Decendents [*sic*]?" An unsigned article in *Montana, the Magazine of Western History* 5 (1955): 36-37.

Wheeler, Olin D. *The Trail of Lewis and Clark, 1804-1904.* rev. ed., 2 vols. New York: G.P. Putnam's Sons, 1926.

Wickman, John E. "Robert Meldrum." In *The Mountain Men and the Fur Trade of the Far West,* 10 vols., edited by LeRoy R. Hafen, 9:279-81. Glendale: Arthur H. Clark Co., 1965-1972.

Wilson, Charles Morrow. *Meriwether Lewis of Lewis and Clark.* New York: Thomas Y. Crowell Co., 1934.

Wilson, Elinor. *Jim Beckwourth: Black Mountain Man and War Chief of the Crows.* Norman: University of Oklahoma Press, 1972.

Zochert, Donald. "'This nation never saw a black man before.'" *American Heritage* 22 (1971): 8-9.

Index

SPECIAL NOTE

Those already interested in the Lewis and Clark Expedition, as well as those who would like to learn more about it, should know of the existence of the Lewis and Clark Trail Heritage Foundation, Inc. Formed to stimulate broader public awareness of the great exploration and its importance to our nation's heritage, the foundation's membership consists of Lewis and Clark enthusiasts from all corners of the country, some of whom have joined together in state and local chapters. In addition to publishing an excellent quarterly entitled *We Proceeded On*, which features highly informative articles about the many fascinating aspects of the Lewis and Clark story, the foundation holds an annual meeting at some appropriate point of interest, usually along the expedition's route. Further information can be obtained by writing to Membership Secretary, Lewis and Clark Trail Heritage Foundation, 5054 S.W. 26th Place, Portland, Oregon 97201.